THE
SHIPPING
FORECAST
PUZZLE BOOK

For my grandpa, Richard Hamilton, who worked at the Met Office and went beyond even Southeast Iceland, carrying out Arctic experiments and noticing some striking things about ozone.

Thank you, from all of us.

THE
SHIPPING
FORECAST
PUZZLE BOOK

Alan Connor

BOOKS

1

BBC Books, an imprint of Ebury Publishing
20 Vauxhall Bridge Road,
London SW1V 2SA

BBC Books is part of the Penguin Random House group
of companies whose addresses can be found at global.
penguinrandomhouse.com

Text © Alan Connor 2020
Design copyright © Woodlands Books 2020

Alan Connor has asserted his right to be identified
as the author of this Work in accordance with
the Copyright, Designs and Patents Act 1988

First published by BBC Books in 2020

www.penguin.co.uk

A CIP catalogue record for this book is available
from the British Library

ISBN 9781785945106

Printed and bound: TBB, a.s. Slovakia

Penguin Random House is committed to a sustainable future for
our business, our readers and our planet. This book is made
from Forest Stewardship Council® certified paper.

CONTENTS

FOREWORD

The Still Small Voice of Calm

The British are an island people but it's easy to forget it, wrapped up in our busy lives. The sea surrounds us; it provides for us, protects us and, try as we might to harness it, it will always remind us that it is an untameable force of nature. It can be savage, spectacular and serene.

I was born in Lowestoft, the same fishing town as the composer Benjamin Britten, whose great work *Peter Grimes* traps the salt air along that stretch of Suffolk coastline in the staves of its score. Generations of my family were fishermen and the susurrating ebb and flow of tides has governed life there for centuries.

Unlike my ancestors, my 20-year professional connection with the sea doesn't get my feet wet, but helps to keep those at sea safe, as a voice of the UK's Shipping Forecast, broadcast four times daily on BBC Radio 4. It is a detailed weather report for seafarers, dividing the waters around the British Isles into 31 areas with curious-sounding names: some are obvious geographical locations such as Dover, Lundy or Hebrides, and others, like Forties and Dogger are more mysterious. Forties is an area of sea consistently 40 fathoms deep and Dogger is a sandbank, named after the *doggers*, medieval Dutch fishing boats.

The forecast gives the wind direction and force, atmospheric pressure, visibility and the state of the sea. It is a nightly litany with a rhythm and indefinable poetry that have made it popular with millions of people who never have cause to put to sea and have little idea what it *actually* means; a reminder that whilst you're tucked up safely under the bedclothes, far out over the waves it's a wilder and more dangerous picture, one that captures the imagination and leads it into unchartered waters whilst you sleep. Dependable, reassuring and never hurried, in these especially uncertain times the Shipping Forecast is a still small voice of calm across the airwaves.

When I began reading the forecast it arrived in the studio via a noisy telex printer that laboriously churned out the data on a roll of very flimsy thermal paper. If the paper ran-out, you had to call the Met Office and ask them to re-send it, which could be perilously close to broadcast. I then had to separate the two-metre-long printout into its constituent parts: Shipping Forecast, Coastal Stations and Inshore Waters by carefully tearing it with a ruler against the desk and fastening each sheet with paperclips to pieces of cereal-box cardboard (kept expressly in the studio for this purpose) so it didn't rustle whilst being read. It was all very endearingly low-tech, just as one would hope.

In this delightful book, Alan Connor embraces all that idiosyncratic history and impishly crafts a cryptic voyage of the mind around each sea area. It is a heroic and highly skilful feat of quizmastery, widening your general and nautical knowledge along the way. The ideal gift for radio lovers, sea dogs and puzzle fiends, and I sincerely hope you enjoy making the journey as much as I have.

Wrap up, it's stormy out there!

Zeb Soanes, London, 2020

WHY WE LOVE THE
SHIPPING FORECAST

'How inappropriate to call this planet Earth
when it is clearly Ocean'

– Arthur C Clarke, in the scientific journal *Nature*

If you're looking at this book in Coton-in-the-Elms –
and as you'll well know, this being your parish's claim
to fame – you're as far from the coast as it's possible to
get in the British Isles. If you're anywhere else, the sea is
at the absolute most 70 miles away, and probably much less.
Depending how you measure it, the British coastline
comes in at a salty 7,723 miles.

Other shores? They're just a day or so's travel away.
In this book, you'll voyage through all the areas covered
by the Shipping Forecast: growing warmer and then
colder, you'll meet and greet our friends in Norway,
Denmark, Germany, the Netherlands, Belgium, France,
Spain, Portugal, Ireland... and back up to Iceland.

You may have visited some of these places for real.
You could, right now, 'visit' any of them by sparking up,
say, Google StreetView. But there exists a world beyond
streets. This book, I hope, opens up the vast areas of
coastline – and of open sea – and lets you experience
them and travel through them. That is, so long as you

know how to handle the waters. Which is where the Shipping Forecast comes in...

On an autumn Tuesday in 1859, the wind off Anglesey did two things.

It changed direction, and it became lethally fierce, reaching force 12 on the Beaufort scale: what we call a hurricane.

In his London home was Bob FitzRoy, former captain of Darwin's *Beagle*, darkly eyeing his barometer. He knew that, in the 1850s, the usual way of anticipating a gale was for a ship's master to look at a frog in a glass case and watch its behaviour (if it waddled up its little ramp: happy weather; if down: perhaps watch out).

Unusually for the era, FitzRoy preferred frogless techniques for flagging up danger. That evening, FitzRoy's barometer dropped ominously. He forecast a disaster.

He was right. The captain of the *Royal Charter*, aiming to complete the last leg of a voyage from Melbourne to Liverpool, pressed on through the wind. The ship was smashed on rocks near Anglesey and 450 people drowned: all the women, all the children and various goldminers who thought they were headed for home. FitzRoy felt helpless... even responsible.

He came up with a novel idea – a 'weather forecast' – and began despatching telegraphs to ports, which displayed warnings in the form of flags that saved life

THE BEAUFORT WIND FORCE SCALE

	Average wind speed in knots (a knot is a little faster than 1mph)	Probable wave height in metres	Description
0	0	less than 1	**Calm**
1	2	0.1	**Light air**
2	5	0.2	**Light breeze**
3	9	0.6	**Gentle breeze**
4	13	1	**Moderate breeze**
5	19	2	**Fresh breeze**
6	24	3	**Strong breeze**
7	30	4	**Near gale**
8	37	5.5	**Gale**
9	44	7	**Strong gale**
10	52	9	**Storm**
11	60	11.5	**Violent storm**
12	more	14 or more	**Hurricane**

after life after life. Come 1924, the newly instituted BBC broadcast the messages: as in, they were literally *cast broadly* to anyone who could receive the signal. (There's more about FitzRoy when you get to the Shipping Area that's named after him.)

Less was – and remains – more in the BBC's Shipping Forecast. Mariners quickly learn the code, and so will you. For each Shipping Area, the first sentence tells you the direction from which the wind will be blowing ('southwest backing east') and how fierce it will be ('4 to 5, increasing 6 later'). The next two describe how you'll find the waves ('rough, occasionally very rough'), and how much rain to expect ('mainly fair'); the last is what kind of visibility to expect ('good', hopefully).

Nigh-on a century later, the BBC still broadcasts the Forecast four times a day. This information, once conveyed by flags, newsprint and posted-up notices, can now be obtained using much more modern kit than a wireless receiver. Still, though, we demand that the Forecast remains on our radios. For some, it's a meaningless aid to falling asleep. For others, it's a poem they love but have no wish to understand. And for all of us, it means something that's very *easy* to understand.

The BBC and the Met Office; the sciences of broadcasting and of meteorology: they work together, day and night, to make sure that any boat, large or small, has a better chance of safe passage.

We'll always look after each other as best we can.
Safe voyages.

· HOW TO PLAY ·

Welcome aboard!

Well, I say that.

You're the one on board. *I'm* the one sending you on a few voyages. Thirty-four voyages, in fact, around all of the Shipping Forecast Areas.

For each Area, you'll see **a map and a set of clues for place names** (bays, islands, undersea features... you'll find them all) somewhere in that map. Using a pencil – or your finger if it's not your own copy – **join those names and trace the shape of a letter** (sometimes a bit wonky).

By the way, the clues don't demand that you're familiar with the places you're visiting. They're a mixture of general knowledge and hints based on what the names look or sound like (especially when we leave these shores and you're being despatched to Icelandic villages or Portuguese coves).

Yes! For every clue, **the answer is there, already written down and waiting for you, somewhere on the map –** which is precisely why many of them are a little, um, playful. And if sometimes you can't immediately recall, say, exactly which Yorkshire resort is troubled by the arrival of Count Dracula, using your phone is *positively* encouraged.

I have no way of knowing who you are, of course. Perhaps you're a real mariner, reading this alone as you traverse German Bight. More likely, you're something like a family looking at the clues together, calling out ideas – and that group approach is what I've tended to presume.

Just occasionally, a clue asks you to tap in some latitude-and-longitude, which is to help those of you who aren't already sailors to feel more like salty mariners.

On that topic... the clues come with little descriptions of your voyages: the sights, the sounds and sometimes the smells. I hope that when you next hear the name of a Shipping Forecast area wafting from your radio, you'll have a richer image of what it's like: whether it's a place of puffins, a channel filled with the eerie honks of container vessels, or both.

Once you've been through every Area – near-African and Icelandic; those with a lot of coast and those where you can never hope to see land – you can assemble those 34 letters to complete a sea shanty. At the end of the book, you'll see how this shanty can earn *you* a Certificate of Maritime Proficiency.

You can make the voyages in any order you like: you can start with a 'Light Breeze' set of clues, or with the place nearest to where you live. I recommend Viking, though, as it helps explain things. Then: go nuts. Anchors aweigh!

In brief:

1. Read the clue.

2. Work out which place in the map it's talking about.

3. Read the next clue.

4. Join the clues in order to form the (wonky) shape of a letter.

5. Sail on to the next area.

'Not for Navigation'

Those three words are ones you see even on very expensive maps of oil fields, even on guides written by seasoned mariners.

They go double, triple, whatever you like, with these puzzles.

You are making voyages in your mind. Some of them may take you to wind farms, over sandbanks and generally to places that boats are advised to avoid.

This book is **not** a navigational aid.

The wavelets around you will grow but never become full. Their crests will break only occasionally.

VIKING

So this voyage is also a kind of *sample*, to introduce you to the things to come. And that includes nautical lingo. When talking about your speed, for example, we'll be using the knot. 'Knot'? What?

A knot is one nautical mile per hour. On land, a mile used to be about a thousand steps (hence the name). At sea, it was a matter of guesswork, until an English mathematician decided that there were 60 nautical miles between each of those horizontal lines of latitude. He was *almost* right, so we've ended up today with a nautical mile being that little bit more than a mile (approximately 1.150779 miles or so, if you insist) – so remember that 40 knots is that little bit faster than 40 mph.

And they're called knots because the old way of keeping tabs on your speed was to count the knots going by on some rope unreeled from boat to water.

Because this is our first voyage, I'll use this introduction to describe how the book works rather than to paint a picture of the area. That's also because Viking – lying between Shetland and the fjords of Norway but not actually reaching either – is an area where, to be blunt, there's not a great deal to describe.

Usually, Viking is a bit of the North Sea you just need to sail right on through – much as the actual Vikings did.

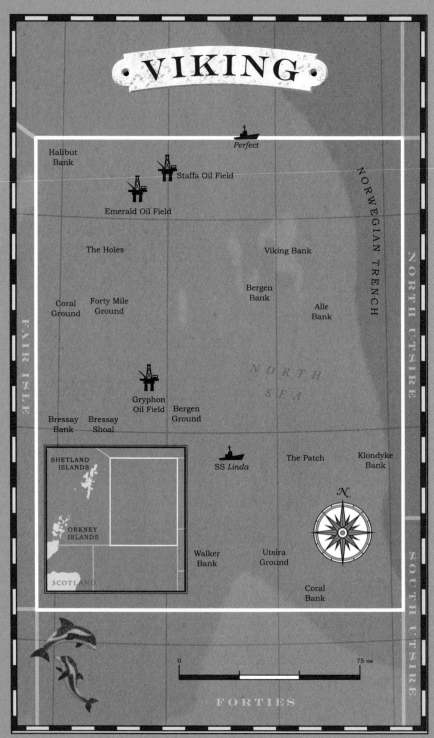

VIKING

Perfect

Halibut
Bank

Staffa Oil Field

Emerald Oil Field

NORWEGIAN TRENCH

NORTH UTSIRE

The Holes

Viking Bank

Bergen
Bank

Coral
Ground

Forty Mile
Ground

Alle
Bank

FAIR ISLE

NORTH
SEA

Gryphon
Oil Field

Bergen
Ground

Bressay
Bank

Bressay
Shoal

SHETLAND
ISLANDS

SS *Linda*

The Patch

Klondyke
Bank

N

ORKNEY
ISLANDS

SCOTLAND

Walker
Bank

Utsira
Ground

SOUTH UTSIRE

Coral
Bank

0   75 NM

FORTIES

MAP 1

Wind Southerly or
southwesterly 2 or 3
Sea state Smooth or slight
Weather Mainly fair
Visibility Good, occasionally poor

START

1. **Complete this rhyme from Robert Browning:**
'Go, cried the Mayor, and get long poles! /
Poke out the nests and block up ___!'

We start with an example of an answer (of two words) that
you're in no way expected to know immediately, but which
will reveal itself with great ease as you peer over the map.
By the way, as you approach your next destination, tack to the
north a little and then later south, so that your journey traces
an outward curve.

2. **It's why where you are is called what it is**

Perhaps an insultingly straightforward question to get us moving,
but there is also wordplay to come (immediately, in fact); curve
outwards to the west a little as you travel south.

3. **Even though we're up by Norway, this name is...**
entirely **in German**

In the other Shipping Areas, these bits in italics won't tend to
describe the shape you're taking, but this is our test run; for now,
take a path to the next point which curves a little to the east.

4. Another quote, this time from Arthur Conan Doyle: '"By Saint Paul!" quoth Sir Nigel, plucking ____ from his eye'

In fact, they will more usually describe what it might be like to actually be on a boat in the relevant Shipping Area (curve a little to the south east, by the way).

5. Yoko, ____, Maureen, Pattie

As you've just seen, we sometimes sail to sunken vessels, which we do with due reverence; curve a little outwards once more.

6. That imaginary creature with the body of a lion and the head of an eagle

You will be thankful for that good visibility as, once again, you curve outwards.

7. One twenty-fifth of a Proclaimer's voyage

And all of these hints to make the shape of your voyage a little more 'round' are probably a big hint, especially when you see that your final destination is...

8. And a final quote, this time from *Antony and Cleopatra*: '... ____ where eyes should be, which pitifully disaster the cheeks' (and yes, we *have* been here *very* recently)

End

· NORTH UTSIRE ·

Not so long ago – at least in Earth terms – this was all un-navigable, because it was all glacier. Then those glaciers started to move, leaving behind them vast valleys thousands of metres deep, often deeper than the seas they feed.

Yes, this is The Fjord One.

Your journey *should* be calm, so long as winds don't funnel in from the mountains; the fjords are *generally* protected from the maelstroms of the North Sea. Be watchful, though, as you round the skerries (those hard little islands also left behind by glaciation).

Jaggedy jaggedy jag.

And do take time to appreciate your proximity to those cold-water coral reefs and their populations which, unlike you, prefer life under enormous pressure and in total darkness.

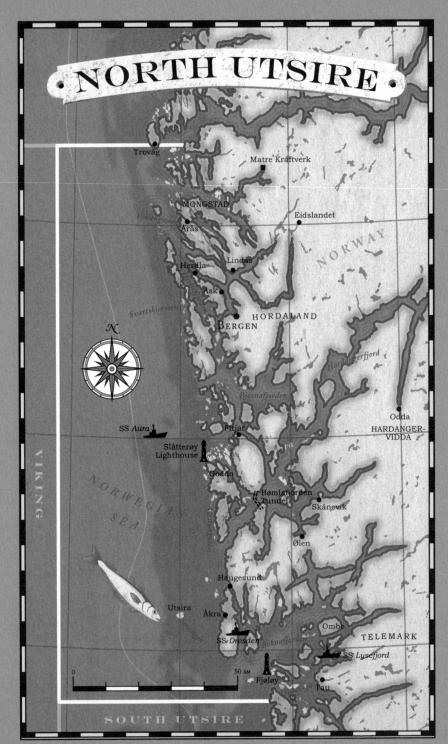

MAP 2

Difficulty
Light breeze

Wind Northerly or northwesterly 2 to 3,
backing westerly 3 to 4 later
Sea state Slight
Weather Good
Visibility Good

START

1. Nolan, Lusardi, Hamilton and Ronstadt

Calmer legs of this voyage await you, but you set out at
an oil terminal with, well, a 10-million-barrel capacity. Tankers,
cargo ships and ro-ro ferries are, it's fair to say, more used to these
channels than you, though you should soon catch sight of the
linden trees – which give your starting point its name – before
heading out into Hjeltefjorden.

2. Kríss Åkabúsi, say?

The atmosphere is different now – almost touristy; the boats you
pass may be leisure fishers, or on their way to bill and coo at that
island's 200+ bird species.

3. New name for Jeeves / Smiths single of 1986 / Pizza chain with 120 outlets

Katabatic (descending) winds may appear from the
fjords without polite warning.

4. Response to getting a 10 from Mr Goodman?

Cross a thoroughfare which goes 142 fathoms below sea level;
meanwhile, the automated Slåtterøy Lighthouse, which has the
most intense light in Norway, gives two flashes every 30 seconds.

5. There was nø point waiting for him, in the end

You'll pass a lighthouse 125 miles above sea level,
which illuminates the entire horizon and can be seen
from 17 miles away.

6. Above which, appropriately, there is plenty of sea *air*

End

· SOUTH UTSIRE ·

In 1984, the various countries which border the North Sea (and which are partial to its fishy foodstuffs) wisely decided that it was in everyone's interest to work with the *same* boundaries for shipping forecasts.

In pursuit of finer detail, the Norwegian coast got *two* areas, each immortalising in its name a tiny island with a name that's very similar to, but *not* identical to 'Utsire': the herring-loving Utsira. And these areas have been part of the Shipping Forecast ever since.

Nautical guides for South Utsire area typically involve great aerial photographs, taken at a tilt, giving navigators another sense of the eye-popping snaking lines that they must imagine between islands and outcrops.

These coasts are popular with tall-ships enthusiasts and sometimes form the arena for awesome races of these vessels: check – *before* you set off – that these monsters won't be swooping along your coastline.

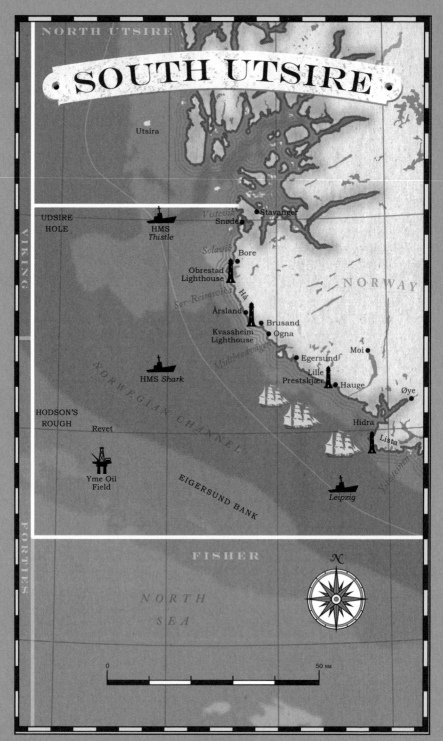

MAP 3

| Difficulty
Strong gale

Wind Southwesterly becoming
cyclonic for a time, 8 to 9 later
Sea state Rough, occasionally
very rough
Weather Thundery showers
Visibility Moderate

START

1. Surely you don't think *I'm* responsible!?

You start in what is technically a lake, one which glacial movement has left so very 'overdeepened' that its depth is sometimes 172 fathoms...

2. 'I praise my ___! It is a small Paris and educates its people' (Goethe's *Faust*)

... but things are now a lot deeper, as you are presently over the incredibly profound Norwegian Trench, which means that you need to be deeply respectful of the potent northeasterly Norwegian Coastal Current.

3. The original hosts, ___ Tess

You'll know you're in the right spot if you can see the hideous stone and concrete bollards which stretch for miles, known locally as Hitler's Teeth; keep yourself on the far side of the Jæren reef.

4. I knew it!

One of the lighthouses produces, as well as its continuous bright white light, a radar-beacon '– – –' in Morse.

5. Not at all! Its point break makes it a *very* exciting surfing spot

It's all getting a bit rocky: rocky enough that these waters have had a piloting service since the mid-1600s: today's pilot vessels are marked LOS.

6. I imagine it *did*, being at the same kind of latitude as the northerly John O'Groats

The Norwegians here are the closest Norwegian landlubbers get to Scotland; you're going to get a little bit closer still, on which topic...

7. Norway is to heather... as... Scotland is to ____

Though you're straying a long way from shore, you will never even get close to the edge of Norway's hard-fought – and very wide – Exclusive Economic Zone.

8. I feel so sorry for myself

End

FORTIES

We have not yet translated 'fathom' into landlubber.
It's six feet (or 1.8 metres, or one and one-eighth Lord
Nelsons). And why are we talking about *this* as we
prepare to head out into Forties?

The bed of the North Sea rises and falls, across and down
– *except* where we are now. This area in the middle, between
Scotland and Scandinavia, but reaching neither, is stubbornly
and persistently forty fathoms deep. Hence all the '40's on
an Admiralty chart of the area and hence the name.

If you look at the Forties area on, say, Google Maps, you
won't see anything of great interest. And not so long ago,
there wasn't much to see apart from those hunting herring.
Since the Second World War, though, various people have
become very interested in what's under that forty-fathom
bed. Hence the wreck of the Piper Alpha oil platform at the
north of the Shipping Area, and the many rigs and vessels
you will be avoiding.

So, check that your NMs (Notices to Mariners) have been
updated and you know the position of mobile rigs. After
dark, platforms should show a white light. And you may not
go nearer than 500m to any rig, any mooring for loading
tankers, or any permanent platform except in an emergency
or extreme weather.

The forecast is fog.

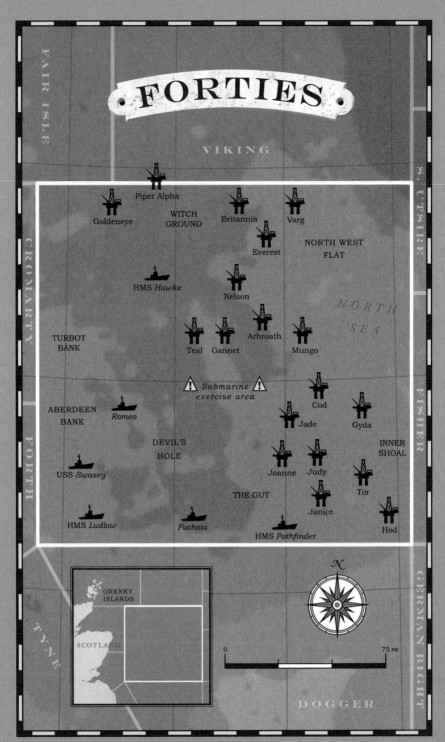

MAP 4

Difficulty
Moderate breeze

Wind Southerly veering southwesterly, 3 or 4
Sea state Mainly slight
Weather Showers
Visibility Poor

START

1. Scarlet, Saffron, Primrose, ____...

Oil types call the area you're over 'the J-Block', for obvious reasons.

2. Out of which the Styx flows?

In pre-glacial times, it seems, the Rhine flowed up to where you are now.

3. Duck!

The platform you're approaching has been there since 1989, and drills to a depth of around 1,800 fathoms.

4. Those caught *here* might be heading *there* for a smoking

... and back across, over where we're draining the Palaeocene oil reservoir ...

5. Since the 1920s, a term for a greedy person, originally a sailor

Now you're over a basin made up of post-glacial clay that gets as much as 40 metres thick.

6. You might hang around here for a spell

And finally, here, we're emptying not only the Palaeocene reservoir, but the Forties and Sandstone too.

7. Uh, *actually*, if you include ones that start underwater, Mauna Kea is a mile taller

End

CROMARTY

This voyage is in the Moray Firth. Do not, on any account, expect to encounter Moray eels. Morays prefer water that is quite different. Water that has reefs. Water that contains *other* Moray eels. Water that is, frankly, warm. This water is not warm. This is Scottish water; most of Cromarty is, anyway. And unlike the west coast, there's only one island of any decent size between John O'Groats and Berwick.

Visibility is often *strikingly* high. You might be off the coast of Nairn, but still able to look across 17 nautical miles over the Cromarty Firth to see the markings of the lighthouse at Tarbat Ness. When you are travelling near the coast, though, a *lot* of what you'll see is cliffs. The port which gives us the word Cromarty has a Gaelic name which means 'the crooked place'.

You'll encounter fishing boats, on the hunt for Norway lobsters (to be clear, that's the name of the beast, *not* the nationality of those who have the legal right to fish for it) and scallops (however you may pronounce that); more traditionally, the area has been harvested for herring – and traditions on the land here last a long time. By way of example, the feudal system here was abolished... in 2004. If you spot Mischief or Spirtle, do wave hello.

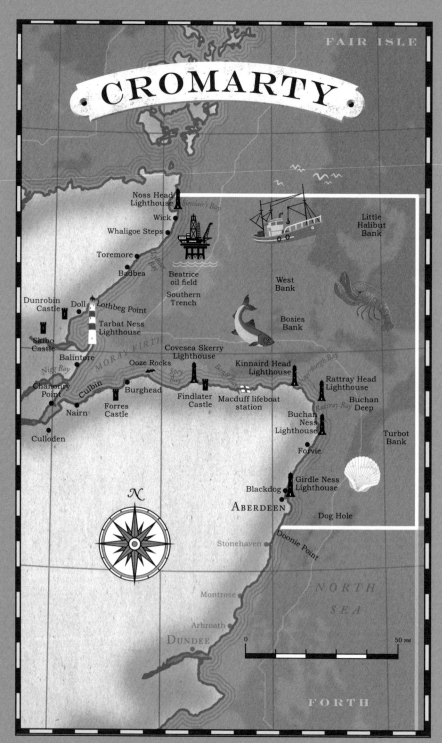

CROMARTY

FAIR ISLE

Noss Head
Lighthouse · *Sinclair Bay*
Wick
Whaligoe Steps

Little
Halibut
Bank

Toremore
Badbea

Beatrice
oil field

West
Bank

Southern
Trench

Dunrobin
Castle · Doll · Lothbeg Point

Bosies
Bank

Skibo
Castle
Balintore
Nigg Bay

Tarbat Ness
Lighthouse

Covesea Skerry
Lighthouse

Kinnaird Head
Lighthouse

Fraserburgh Bay

Rattray Head
Lighthouse

MORAY FIRTH

Ooze Rocks
Spey Bay

Banff Bay

Buchan
Deep

Chanonry
Point

Culbin

Burghead

Findlater
Castle

Macduff lifeboat
station

Rattray Bay

Nairn

Forres
Castle

Buchan
Ness
Lighthouse

Turbot
Bank

Culloden

Forvie

Girdle Ness
Lighthouse

Blackdog

ABERDEEN

Dog Hole

N

Stonehaven · Doonie Point

NORTH
SEA

Montrose

Arbroath

DUNDEE

0   50 NM

FORTH

MAP 5

Difficulty	
Strong breeze / moderate gale	

Wind Southwest backing east or
northeast, 6 or 7
Sea state Mainly slight
Weather Showers
Visibility Moderate

START

1. Stately home for a king who's no longer puttin' on his ermine?

Stay close to the coast that was once known as the verdant Granary of Moray until the Great Sand Drift of 1694 created a Scottish desert.

2. Half of a title that has taken Cliff Richard to number one, twice

Now sail along the coast: you will see crofts where some of the victims of the Highland Clearances put out to sea from these shores in search of herring, some of them ascending and descending a colossal manmade stairway to do so.

3. A wicked thing always has one

You are now leaving a port which entered the twenty-first century in decline, having lost 80 per cent of its fishing income, now with a handsome new pontoon to lure 'leisure mariners... such as yourself; next will come the highest waves of your journey; also, check your stern to see that your country-of-origin flag is intact and visible...

4. There's another one on the Dead Sea

You're now over a fault line, which is not unconnected to the site you've just visited; you'll be getting closer to the Forties shipping area before you'll see dry land again.

5. A very, very short rave review, celebrating the complexity of *The Thirty-Nine Steps*?

Soon after you re-enter UK waters, you will be passing the site of Duncan's castle in *Macbeth* – and the nearby heath where the witches kick things off.

6. It was named after the wife of a man worth half a billion dollars

Two things to watch out for on this leg: the first is the delightful sight of Mischief, Spirtle and the rest of the Moray Firth's population of bottlenose dolphins; the second is that, as you pass the point where the south-south-west stream dissolves, you are technically bordering a 25-mile-long zone officially defined as a Military Danger Area (as in, it's used for firing practice), and there's a bunch of unexploded ordnance if you stray north too soon.

7. What a victim of a sting operation might be heard to say

End

FORTH

Having consulted their own version of the Shipping
Forecast (that is, gazing at their enormous skyscapes), the
Vikings sailed into what is now the Forth shipping area in
793 and set about assailing the islanders in the Firth and
smashing up Holy Island.

Twelve centuries later, these shores are seeing another
invasion, this time from New Zealand. Inadvertently
smuggled among imported wool: a dwarf plant, the piri
piri burr, which enjoys the sandy dunes of these coasts
and which is playing havoc with Holy Island's plant life
(not to mention the coats of local dogs).

Longboats and trading vessels: Forth – the river's name
means 'the slow-flowing one' – is home to big craft. There
are seals here, and puffins, but you will be spending your
time in busy shipping routes; this will be no bucolic jaunt.

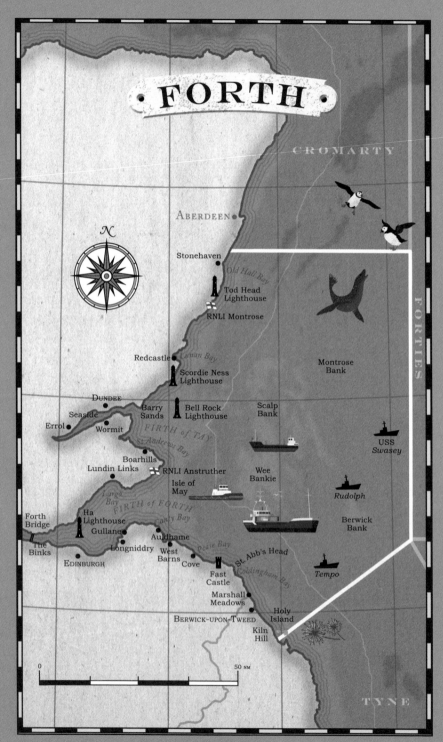

FORTH

CROMARTY

FORTIES

ABERDEEN

Stonehaven

Old Hall Bay

Tod Head
Lighthouse

RNLI Montrose

Lunan Bay

Redcastle

Scordie Ness
Lighthouse

Montrose
Bank

DUNDEE

Seaside

Barry
Sands

Bell Rock
Lighthouse

Scalp
Bank

Errol

Wormit

FIRTH of TAY

St Andrews Bay

USS
Swasey

Boarhills

Lundin Links

RNLI Anstruther

Isle of
May

Wee
Bankie

Rudolph

*Largo
Bay*

Forth
Bridge

Ha
Lighthouse

FIRTH of FORTH

Canty Bay

Berwick
Bank

The
Binks

Gullane

Auldhame

Longniddry

West
Barns

Peffer Bay

St. Abb's Head

EDINBURGH

Cove

Coldingham Bay

Tempo

Fast
Castle

Marshall
Meadows

Holy
Island

BERWICK-UPON-TWEED

Kiln
Hill

0   50 NM

TYNE

MAP 6

Difficulty
Moderate breeze

Wind Southerly 3, occasionally 4
Sea state Mainly slight
Weather Occasional showers
Visibility Good, occasionally
moderate

START

1. Actually, no one has done that to it since 2011

Even if northerlies cause a violent swell, you must not try to take shelter in Mortimer's Deep, as it is a gas terminal and any vessel needs permission from the Navigation Service; Rosyth is your port of call in an emergency...

2.

When peregrine falcons appear in these parts, looking for food, thousands of other birds often flee from shore, filling the sky in mere moments.

3. Presumably three-quarters of the inhabitants are bulls and the rest are twins

As you leave, you will notice marked areas: avoid them and you will also avoid disturbing seals that are moulting or trying to breed with a modicum of dignity.

4. It may well be, but still: don't scrape your bottom on it

The entrance here is dangerous in easterlies, southeasterlies and when there's a big old onshore swell...

5. What to do if your pet has an itchy tummy

... and the depths on your charts should be taken with a pinch of salt; there are strong tidal streams around here...

6. Anagram of 'disease' and actually a *fairly* on-the-nose spot of naming

... oh yes, and be sure not to let your keel get stuck in the mud.

7. His roles included Fletcher, Juan and, notably, Robin

Before it was possible to build the lighthouse you were about to pass, many ruses were tried to help passing traffic, including a decidedly old-school actual bell, maintained by abbots from Arbroath and tolled by the movement of the waves.

8. Don't hang about here or things might get hairy

End

TYNE

The sea stretches out 400 nautical miles to the east, all the way to the Syddanmark coasts of Scandinavia. Happily, the Tyne area – your playground for now – doesn't extend *too* far from shore.

In earlier days of the Shipping Forecast, the information for the Tyne area was of great interest to those arriving at and leaving these shores for the *phenomenal* amount of shipbuilding that took place on Tyne – and indeed Wear – since around 1346.

At the end of the nineteenth century, the focus moved from wooden ships to iron hulls. The next century started with RMS *Mauretania* and RMS *Carpathia* (the one that rescued passengers from RMS *Titanic*); by 1980, there were two shipyards left, which merged to make one, which closed in 1988.

Nowadays, many of your neighbours in the wilder reaches of Tyne will be involved with oil and gas. But for the most part, you will be following in the wake of more familiar figures: monks and vampires, heroes from Shakespeare and even some from real life.

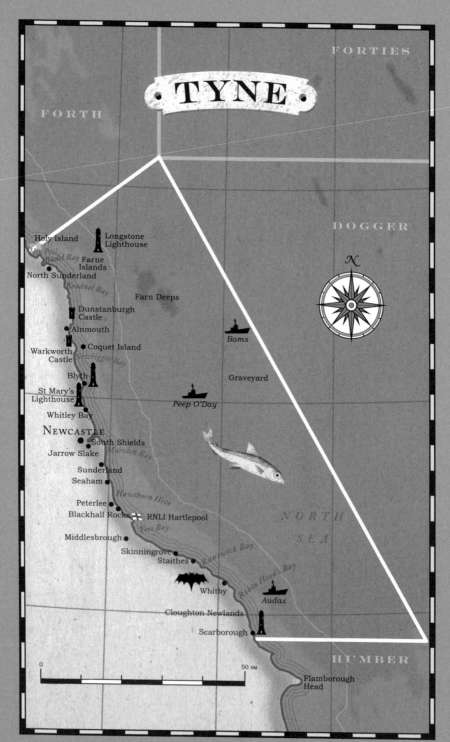

FORTIES

FORTH

TYNE

DOGGER

Holy Island
Longstone
Lighthouse
Budel Bay
Farne
Islands
North Sunderland
Beadnel Bay
Farn Deeps
Dunstanburgh
Castle
Alnmouth
Bams
Warkworth
Castle
Coquet Island
Newbiggin Bay
Blyth
Graveyard
St Mary's
Lighthouse
Peep O'Day
Whitley Bay
NEWCASTLE
South Shields
Jarrow Slake
Mursden Bay
Sunderland
Seaham
Hawthorn Hive
Peterlee
Blackhall Rocks
RNLI Hartlepool
NORTH
Tees Bay
Middlesbrough
SEA
Skinningrove
Staithes
Runswick Bay
Whitby
Robin Hood's Bay
Audax
Cloughton Newlands
Scarborough
HUMBER
0   50 NM
Flamborough
Head

MAP 7

Difficulty
Fresh breeze

Wind Northeast backing west,
5 occasionally 6
Sea state Slight or moderate
Weather Mainly fair
Visibility Good

START

1.

The watchkeeper (VHF channel 12) may help you avoid
the coastal defences around Castle Headland, just north
of the harbour.

**2. Place name you'd probably expect to find in
Nottinghamshire, if Nottinghamshire weren't
quite so landlocked**

The protection offered by the marshy moors around this inlet
made this bay a haunt for those who saw that smuggling tea,
tobacco and gin would be more lucrative than fishing; to get
to the marina you're headed for, know that the swing bridge
opens by request.

3. Abbey by which Dracula's ship runs aground

You pass an extraordinary nature reserve where seals, wading
birds and some astonishing flora insist on surviving with the
steelworks, nuclear power station and oil, gas and chemical
plants which have joined them along the mouth of the river...

4. **They received an apology from Wembley for spelling their name with an irritating extra vowel**

... and, as you pass Easington, take a moment to imagine the scene a generation or so ago, when the collieries spat out slag, sewage and great eerie orange rocks on to the coastline...

5. **291 miles from Hyde Park, which you'd notice if you were one of the ones making that journey on foot**

... now, on your port side, you can see the castle depicted in Shakespeare's *Henry IV* and its sequel (on land) and hopefully also see some dolphins (in the water); you are not actually permitted to land at your next stop, in line with the policy of the owners since 1972 (unless you happen to be a bird).

6. **The female version is used more often now, but men can be flirts too**

Next, you'll pass some resorts patronised by posh Victorian Newcastlers, for this here is Kipper Country...

7. **You're suggesting the city centre extends for *60 miles*?**

... their forefathers, the Newcastle merchants, were too greedy to pay for the upkeep of a lighthouse here; when the Forfarshire was shipwrecked in 1838, young Grace Darling and her family saved nine lives and she has been rightly celebrated in song and book ever since.

8. They had one of the UK's biggest-selling albums of 1972, then a quiet period before getting to number two in 1990 with a midfielder from Gateshead

Long before the lighthouse, boats carrying limestone and coal used to mistake Emmanuel Head for the Lind channel, and so a 48-foot (14.6-metre) pyramid was constructed here and painted a suitably striking shade of white.

9. Because the kind of people who give names to marine features *don't* mess around

If you're looking for a prominent point to help with navigation, the meteorological mast and two massive towers of the windfarm might just help.

10. It sounds like they're happy to have a lighthouse here

End

Large waves are starting to appear.
There are extensive white foam crests
all around your vessel, and you
will encounter some spray.

DOGGER

For an area with no land, Dogger looms large in the mind.

First, there's that name. Dogger the Shipping Area is named after Dogger the sandbank, which is named after *dogger*, the Dutch kind of fishing boat, which is named after *dogge*... which means 'cod'. Dogger has long been about fish.

And then there's the prehistory. Named after all of the above is Doggerland.

For years, geophysicists have taken a great interest whenever a fishing boat has dredged up human bones from the seabed around these parts. More bones than can be accounted for by mariners. And that antler found by a trawler in the 1930s *certainly* can't be accounted for by mariners.

Scottish scientists have managed to persuade the oil companies who now inhabit Dogger to gather both fossils and data to build up a picture of what Doggerland was like... before there was any sea there.

You're sailing over ancient tree stumps that have stubbornly survived, pieces of flint that were once people's tools and the occasional mammoth. Doggerland was once the heart of Europe, when you could walk from the Ouse to the Rhine. It's a kingdom lost, 8,000 years ago, to rising sea levels.

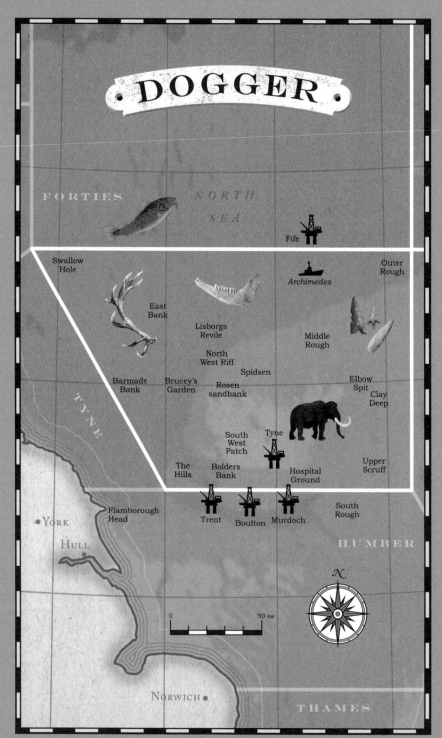

MAP 8

Difficulty
Moderate gale

Wind South 6 to gale 7, veering west
Sea state Rough, becoming moderate
or rough later
Weather Rain then squally showers
Visibility Poor

START

1. Closer to the cranium than to the clavicle, then?

There is a preponderance of sprats below and around your boat...

2. Complimentary response to Muhammad Ali's poetry, before 1964?

... now the area is often teeming with ling...

3. You can't sail over it. You can't sail under it. Oh no! You've got to sail past it!

... here, it's plaice...

4. For the same reason, there is pasta with the same name

... now it's not 'fish'-fish, but eels...

5. She was – ironically – named after someone who understood buoyancy very well

... or rather, for all of the above, there should be those creatures, allowing for over-fishing.

6. They're alive at the start of the movie

End

FISHER

No prizes, sadly, if you've solved the mystery of the reason for the name of this Shipping Area, although those fishers have fished for fish here so voraciously that your voyage will nowadays involve very little mingling with, say, trawlers, their nets having largely moved to the Baltic – for at least as long as *those* waters provide a lucrative catch.

If you catch the winds that *this* part of the sea is known for, and if you take account of its relatively unintimidating tides, this little area – while not a breeze – should be one of your happier voyages.

And please do spare any fish you might spot, and leave their delicious bodies for the Porbeagle sharks. Those gentle beasts need that plaice.

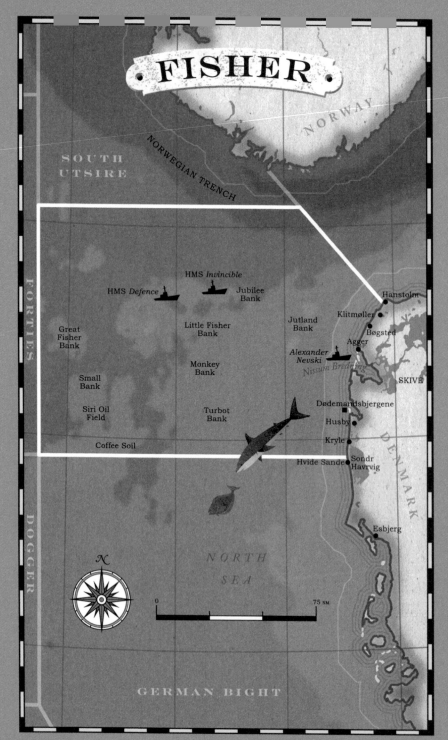

FISHER

NORWAY

SOUTH
UTSIRE

NORWEGIAN TRENCH

FORTIES

HMS *Invincible*

HMS *Defence*

Jubilee
Bank

Great
Fisher
Bank

Little Fisher
Bank

Jutland
Bank

Hanstolm

Klitmøller

Bøgsted

Agger

*Alexander
Nevski*

Nissum Bredning

SKIVE

Monkey
Bank

Small
Bank

Siri Oil
Field

Turbot
Bank

Dødemandsbjergene

Husby

Kryle

Hvide Sande

Sondr
Havrvig

DENMARK

Coffee Soil

Esbjerg

N

NORTH
SEA

0   75 NM

DOGGER

GERMAN BIGHT

MAP 9

Difficulty
Light breeze

Wind North 2 to 4
Sea state Mainly slight
Weather Fair
Visibility Good

START

1. Does *anyone* in this part of Denmark do
any work?

There's not much of a tidal stream for you to factor in; as you
head out to larger waters, the buildings will rapidly become
hidden, as sandbanks fill the view from behind.

2. Perhaps there's a £500 fee to sail here?

Some words that might prove useful in case you need to
spark up your radio: regn (rain)...

3. It shares a name with Tiny's bigger brother,
the son of Major and Granny and friend of the
Soup Dragon

... ankerplads (anchorage)...

4. According to *Gardeners' Question Time*, a
wonderful way to deter slugs and to niftily
darken your compost

...and byge (squall).

5. 'Hey', given the lack of wifi around here, 'she' is unlikely to be a great deal of help

As you head back in the direction you'd take to land, remember that it is always, in a sense, getting slightly further away: up to 11 metres a year, thanks to the persistent lapping of the waves.

6. The _____ War: 1995 dispute between Spain and Canada over fishing rights

End

GERMAN BIGHT

The name suggests that you'll need to have your paperwork in order for docking in German ports; in *fact* you'll be in Danish and Dutch waters as well.

Seafaring has a long history in these parts: graduates of the navigation school established in the North Frisian Islands in the 1600s became sought after far, *far* beyond these shores.

Their maps, however brilliant, would be of no use today. What were once islands are often now part of the mainland and much of the land you'll be travelling alongside – and between – has been reclaimed, rebuilt or otherwise transmogrified from sea to *terra firma*.

So, you've got sandy shallows that can change without warning, frontal systems that can do likewise and three different nations' protocols to follow. Perhaps try to summon the attention-to-detail spirit of those North Frisian pioneers.

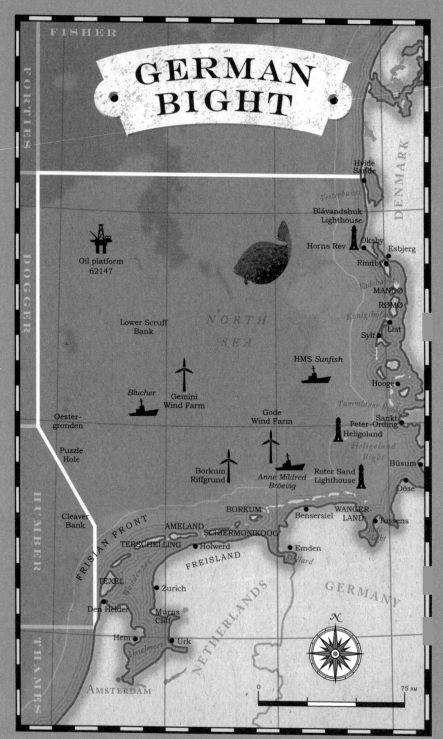

GERMAN BIGHT

FISHER

FORTIES

DOGGER

HUMBER

THAMES

DENMARK

Hvide Sande

Vesterhavet

Blåvandshuk Lighthouse

Horns Rev

Oksby

Esbjerg

Rindby

Oil platform 62147

Vadehavet

MANDØ

RØMØ

Kongishavet

List

Lower Scruff Bank

NORTH SEA

Sylt

HMS *Sunfish*

Hooge

Tummlaner Bucht

Blucher

Gemini Wind Farm

Sankt Peter-Ording

Oester-gronden

Gode Wind Farm

Heligoland

Heligoland Bight

Büsum

Puzzle Hole

Borkum Riffgrund

Anne Mildred Bröevig

Roter Sand Lighthouse

Döse

Cleaver Bank

BORKUM

Bensersiel

WANGER-LAND

Tossens

FRISIAN FRONT

AMELAND

SCHIERMONIKOOG

TERSCHELLING

Holwerd

Emden

Dollard

FREISLAND

GERMANY

TEXEL

Waddenzee

Zurich

NETHERLANDS

Den Helder

Murns Cliff

Urk

N

Hem

Isselmeer

AMSTERDAM

0   75 KM

MAP 10

Difficulty
Moderate breeze

Wind Southerly 2 to 3
Sea state Moderate,
occasionally slight
Weather Mainly fair
Visibility Good

START

1. What Mr. Watts did when Angie asked 'im to dance

You're starting at a destination for some vessels in Humber.

2. Partner of 'haw' that isn't 'hee'

There are potent tidal streams, and then immediately a bunch of shipping vessels and ferries in a mad commercial hurry to further-off waters.

3. This old fishing village sounds annoying

... so be very aware of the depths.

4. It has approximately 1,520,778 fewer inhabitants than its namesake

You're approaching the base of the local Royal Navy and they are very much in charge of the Marinehaven.

5. Castor, but not oil

In strong westerlies, the sea level can rise four metres around these parts.

6. No, not dëse

When you get in to the approach channel, do remember to sound one long blast to ask for the lock to be opened.

7. A place to catch up with your büddies?

Be aware that when the channels divide around here, sometimes one prong of some fork will lead you to... much sand.

8. But it's less than three miles, end to end!

The island you're approaching has become overrun by German superstars; in other words, watch out for wallies on jet-skis.

9. Amazingly, it *doesn't* mean 'mud which has been carried by water'

There are no harbour lights, so rely on buoys for your navigation.

10. What a boat may do in a strong westerly, for example

There are channels dredged here for your convenience; you'll note from the orientation of the thatched-roof homes that westerlies very much predominate here.

11. 'I hope you've pared all that lemon ___ the time I've finely grated this garlic' (comment while preparing *gremolata*, perhaps)

End

HUMBER

The official coordinates for Humber place its southeast corner at 52°45'N and 04°40'E. This means that two and a half miles of Dutch coast just sneak in. And it's a beach. I'm telling you this because this means that the easternmost third of Humber is Dutch waters, and *that* means that you're forbidden from emptying your loo once you get past the third meridian.

On neither side of the area do things tend to go much above the flat. Sky and sea meet and stay met. The stories Humber has to tell, though, are *far* from flat. The Humber itself (strictly an estuary shared by the Ouse and the Trent rather than an actual river) is probably named after the ungentle Humber the Hun, who invaded these shores about 30 centuries ago. The skeleton in Skegness's cupboard is, the locals say, an actual skeleton in an actual cupboard, still wearing the uniform of a customs officer decades after being locked in by smugglers.

These waters have long connected rather than divided the lands on either side: Blakeney (England's fourth most important port until the boats got bigger) was known not only for Dutch gin, legally imported or otherwise, but also for the locals speaking the Dutch language.

And today, ready or not, you're going to recreate those links.

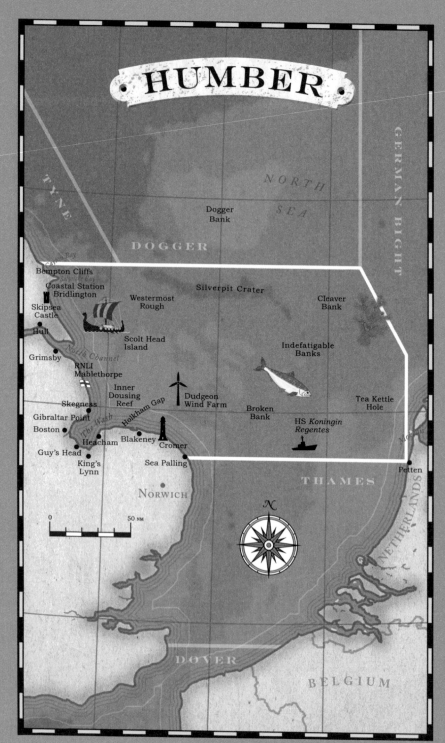

HUMBER

NORTH SEA

GERMAN BIGHT

Dogger
Bank

DOGGER

Silverpit Crater

Cleaver
Bank

Bempton Cliffs
Coastal Station
Bridlington

Westermost
Rough

Skipsea
Castle

Hull

Scolt Head
Island

North Channel

Indefatigable
Banks

Grimsby

RNLI
Mablethorpe

Inner
Dousing
Reef

Holkham Gap

Dudgeon
Wind Farm

Tea Kettle
Hole

Skegness

Gibraltar Point

The Wash

Broken
Bank

Boston

Heacham

Blakeney

Cromer

HS *Koningin
Regentes*

Guy's Head

King's
Lynn

Sea Palling

Petten

NORWICH

THAMES

NETHERLANDS

0   50 NM

N

DOVER

BELGIUM

MAP 11

Difficulty
Strong breeze

Wind Southwesterly 4 to 5,
increasing 6 later
Sea state Moderate,
occasionally rough
Weather Showers
Visibility Moderate

START

1. Its name used to refer to the *adjacent* chess piece, before it got an upgrade

The sandbanks around here don't tend to stay in the same place, but the buoys get moved around to keep you away from them.

2. Its nickname rhymes with 'eggy', as in 'Personally I'd give me right ball for a week in ____' (Bert in *The Growing Pains of Adrian Mole*)

As you leave, keep a look out on port side for the cloud-watchers on the shore by Anderby Creek. The locals say that, while the official charts indicate strong streams here, they tend to underestimate the sheer power of the water: do with that information what you will as you arrive.

3. Anagram of 'Special Steaks'

Look behind you and take in the cliffs at Mappleton. No, your eyes do not deceive you. This is a place where England is simply falling into the sea.

4. Place to sail past in a cutter?

The coast here is low, and may not be visible from seaward, so do please use the chimneys of that power station to guide you in.

5. After six goldfishes and three gerbils 'went to live on a farm', we wearily moved on to ____

You will wish to avoid wherever today's densest areas of commercial traffic are, which may involve some light meandering.

6. Well, you wouldn't be able to pour if it *didn't* have one

Obviously you're not allowed to go all the way to your next destination...

7. What other names did they consider? Gall? Ire? Umbrage?

When the wind farms are under (re-)construction, their outermost points are pointed out, for your safety, by cardinal marks.

8. Bar-tailed godwits? Yes, in the winter. Ringed plover? Check, all year round. Barbary apes? Um, no

End

THAMES

The water the Thames spews out may not be the world's most wholesome, but it has improved since 1959, when the Natural History Museum declared the Thames not merely polluted but 'biologically dead'.

That dirty water you're navigating didn't used to be here, of course: not in the days when Britain was part of mainland Europe, when the Thames and Rhine met in a colossal lake, its outflow not far from where you are now.

Today, this area includes three countries (OK, four, for those of you who include the Principality of Sealand, an offshore anti-aircraft gun platform declared a microstate in 1975, where Ed Sheeran holds the title of baron).

So there are different rules to learn and to follow. Keep 50 metres from those wind turbines along the Netherlands coast, for example. Half a kilometre from the transformer platforms. Don't try to anchor or even touch the seabed in their vicinity and for goodness' sake, don't get out a fishing net.

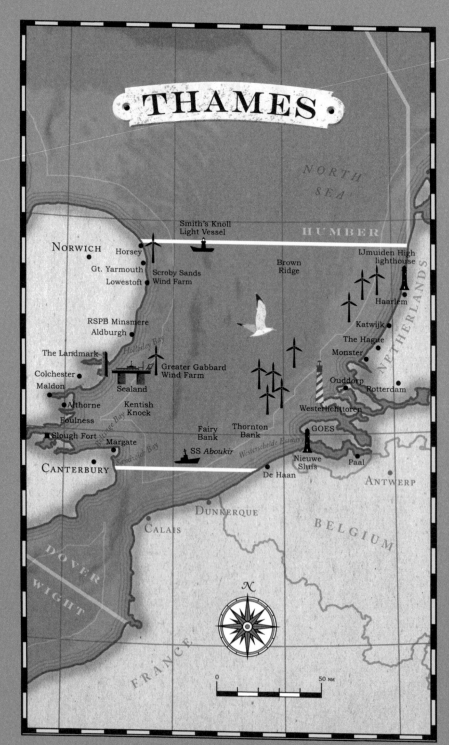

MAP 12

Wind Southeast 4 or 5, veering
east 5 to 6.
Sea state Moderate becoming
moderate or rough
Weather Rain
Visibility Good, occasionally poor

START

1. Beach that shares a name with what you might take there

North of you are the ferries crossing to and from Oostende; to the south, those crossing to and from Dunkerque – meaning that before long, you'll be crossing a heavy traffic lane.

2. Town you'll be familiar with, depending on your cultural tastes, from an essay by Charles Lamb, the film *Mr Turner*, Tracey Emin's home-cum-studio, the novel *Last Orders* or a knees-up by Chas 'n' Dave

If you see a load of oystercatchers, little egrets, avocets and Brent geese headed in one direction, they're making for your destination (or, it must be admitted, away from it).

3. 'It is no vicious blot, murder, or ____ ... that hath depriv'd me of your grace and favour' (Cordelia in *King Lear*)

Worth knowing about here: a five-nautical-mile tongue which extends for another three in the form of a spit.

4. A foodstuff from here has been stocked at Harrods since 1900 and was awarded the Royal Warrant in 2012

Use the buoys to make sure you disturb neither the numerous lobster pots nor the extensive oyster beds.

5. I'm absolutely *not* saying that the good people of Essex are unimaginative when they're thinking up names for prominent spots along the coast...

You can now see the entrance to a backwater which Arthur Ransome declared his favourite place to take his yacht, which has been preserved by a trust which believes that 'everyone should have the unique experience of being onboard or sailing the Nancy Blackett'.

6. Where you might have a mare with a stud?

Day shapes are strongly enforced in this country: so make sure there's a – dangling from your mast if you're motor-sailing and a – when you're at anchor.

7. Anything ____

Like your previous, your next destination is not a port of entry... so... don't enter.

8. Don't be alarmed: it probably got that name because there was a building there with a load of monks in

... and if there's any red diesel in your tanks, you need evidence that the duty has been paid (we're talking receipts).

9. One of those cities that you might think is a capital, seeing as it's a judicial *and* political centre *and* has the foreign embassies, *and* is where the monarchy does its business... but for some reason *isn't* the capital

And now is a good moment to consult your copy of *Waterstanden & Stromen*, a table of tides which – like the marinas and rescue services around here – is obligingly English-speaking.

10. A very similarly named part of New York reminds us how far the Dutch sailed from these shores

End

We are at the larger end of waves
that remain wavelets and their crests
are breaking with glassy foam.
You will probably see scattered
white horses.

· DOVER ·

This is the smallest area you'll be visiting. That may make it sound like the navigation will be straightforward. It is also, however, the world's busiest shipping channel.

Since more than 400 vessels cross the Straits of Dover every day, your journey will be *in no sense* relaxing, though hopefully you can stave off what Matthew Arnold called 'the eternal note of sadness' in his poem 'Dover Beach'.

You'll see the White Cliffs, of course, but there will be no time to commune with nature. In addition, any boat crossing the Channel needs a passage plan; without one, you can be prosecuted if an accident should occur. You're going to be in *three* different territorial waters, so do try to keep on top of your paperwork.

And you may wish to reflect on the rich history of these straits, although, as the place where the British Isles are closest to the mainland, the legacy is mainly of invasion and incursion.

On the other hand, Bexhill-on-Sea was the first place, in 1901, to allow 'mixed' bathing, so it's not *all* stressful.

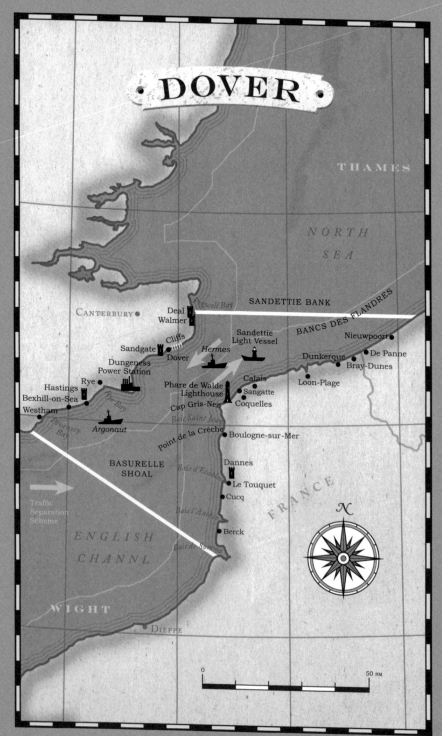

MAP 13

Difficulty
Gentle / moderate breeze

Wind East veering southwest, 2 to 3
Sea state Mainly slight
Weather Rain later
Visibility Good

START

1. Location for the most lucrative Second World War film ever made (2017, co-starring Harry Styles)

As you leave harbour, steer well clear of Charles de Gaulle Lock: this is where the incredibly large ships hulk their way in and out.

2. *Actually,* boats have been coming and going here for over a thousand years

Do you see the lighthouse? It's probably worth knowing that a bearing of 294° from that marks the edge, for 12 nautical miles, of a firing range. Call the range officer on channel 67 if you're at all concerned (which you should be).

3. Castle whose existence was repeatedly questioned by Noel Edmonds

The huge undersea chalk platform here was crossable in the heyday of the hovercraft but has repeatedly been deeply unkind to ships.

4. The point on the English coast closest to mainland European (you can do this by eye)

Do check whether the large swim zone by the enormous port you're passing is in force...

5. Now, just for fun, sail directly over one end of the Channel Tunnel...

You are also pretty much following the route of a planned suspension bridge, in a proposal sent to the government in 1981; the engineers conceded that the 15 pylons the road bridge would have needed might have made things somewhat difficult for shipping...

6. ... to the other

When you pass the Phare de Walde lighthouse, you've crossed what the International Hydrographic Organization has agreed is the end of the North Sea. See ya!

7. To keep the child somewhere safe so's mummy can have half an hour to herself, thanks for asking

In the real world, you would be strongly advised against crossing the narrow and busy Traffic Separation Scheme, especially as Dover is notorious for its funnelling southwesterly winds mocking your navigation plans.

8. Surely they can't have expected to find the Golden Fleece in the Straits of Dover?

You're now approaching a huge reserve dedicated to biodiversity management and, even here in the water, you might, if you're lucky, see a harbour porpoise.

9. Port featured in the Bayeux Tapestry under the heading ISTE JUSSIT UT FODERETUR CASTELLUM AT HESTENGA

A conspicuous onshore wind farm is among the marks that might prove helpful.

10. Bitter sounding

You remember, at the start of your journey, having to avoid a firing range? You're approaching another. Keep south of the Stephenson Shoal!

11. They said it would close down in 2018, but it didn't

End

The edges of the crests of the waves
are breaking into spindrift.
Foam blows in well-marked streaks
along the direction of the wind.

WIGHT

At the eastern end of the Wight area are the Seven Sisters cliffs, used in many films for the White Cliffs of Dover because the real thing, being protected, is getting greener, while the Seven Sisters remain the colour everyone imagines the White Cliffs to be.

At the other end is Swanage, with the 40-tonne Portland-stone Globe and the inscription SEAS BUT JOIN THE NATIONS THEY DIVIDE: in this case, Britain to Brittany.

Between them is Wight itself (it means 'the Place of the Division'), so mighty that it breaks each of the day's two incoming tidal waves into a pair, which means that, up in Southampton, you end up with *four* high tides every day. So use buoys and other markers for your pilotage – if, that is, you're going to Southampton. Are you?

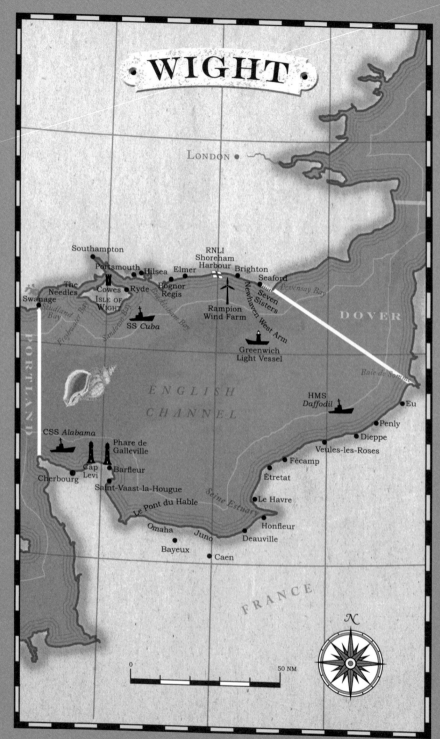

MAP 14

Difficulty
Fresh gale

Wind Southwest 4 to 6, increasing 7
or gale 8
Sea state Rough, occasionally
moderate at first
Weather Rain or thundery showers
Visibility Good, becoming moderate
or poor for a time

START

1. 'Hale knew, before he had been in ____ three hours,
   that they meant to kill him.' (Graham Greene)

Staying with the literary theme, you'll pass where Oscar Wilde divided
his time between *The Importance of Being Earnest* (he named its main
character after the town) and 'getting to know' the locals.

2. He painted himself grey to fit in

Watch out for kayakers, windsurfers and all the rest of them.

3. Town which added a word to its name to celebrate that
   George V had been made to stay there, at around the
   same time that the same monarch reportedly said
   something *incredibly* rude about it

What a harbour you're approaching! Enormous enough that there
is always shelter from the wind to be found somewhere. Since it's
also a naval base, you are now under the careful watch of the
Queen's Harbourmaster.

4. Where you might see Sheila – or Elisha – in a tizzy?

Keep an eye out for the hovercrafts flitting between the pier and
the marina.

5. Town which inspired the line before the line 'And she don't care'

You are approaching the most conveniently placed harbour in the Solent, and one of the most prestigious ports full stop: to avoid the large shoal known as the Shrape Mud, keep outside of a line from the Old Castle buoy to the castle of the Royal Yacht Squadron (yes, as just stated, this is one fancy place).

6. '____ Castle, the Regatta Beating to Windward' (J.M.W. Turner)

The tidal streams are mighty here. The rates off the Prince Consort buoy (a cardinal marker, which tells you which direction is the safe one) can get up to four knots just after High Water Portsmouth, and if you're near the chain ferry during an ebb tide, the rates can get higher. If you're using GPS to measure your speed, keep the tidal stream in mind and do not exceed the local limit (six knots). Once you're past all that, keep an eye out for Glanville fritillary butterflies, which used to be seen way up in Lincolnshire, but tragically can only now be spotted around these parts.

7. The one which was actually shaped like that collapsed in 1764... but they kept the name

You'll know when you're passing by Knoll Beach, as that's the one where no one's wearing swimming costumes.

8. Good inlet to see dreamboats?

It's a long leg now. Plan a harbour of refuge in the event of bad weather or gear failure.

9. The 1992 treaty signed at 50°50′59″N, 5°41′35″E should *really* have been signed here

Strong westerlies here can create a combination of rough water just above patches of shoal.

10. Port whose name means 'the Port'

Use two chimneys and the tower of St Joseph's church for navigation.

11. The time and the place are named after the same Roman deity

You're now passing various fortifications erected by the French – for good reason...

12. When the Cotentin Peninsula is seen as a snail's head, this is the right eye

End

There are small wavelets for now;
their glassy crests will break later.

PORTLAND

Portland is bordered on the north by a good stretch of Jurassic coast. This was *the* place to be 185 million years ago. If you're tempted to disembark for a spot of fossil-hunting, bear in mind what happened when some fishermen dug a hole in Holworth Cliff in 1826. They released a furious heat from the bituminous material below, setting the land on fire for months, which is why you can see the name Burning Cliff marked on your map.

To the south is the coast of Brittany. The closeness of France is why you can see, for example, Corfe Castle as you travel through the Portland area: it's one of many strongholds built by William the Conqueror to ensure no one else could pop across the Channel and do any subsequent conquering. And between the British Isles and France, in many senses, are the Channel Islands.

Oh, and let's not forget the lighthouse which shares a name with the area: Portland Bill, currently being renovated with a green (as in eco, not as in colour) LED lamp with a reach of 18 nautical miles.

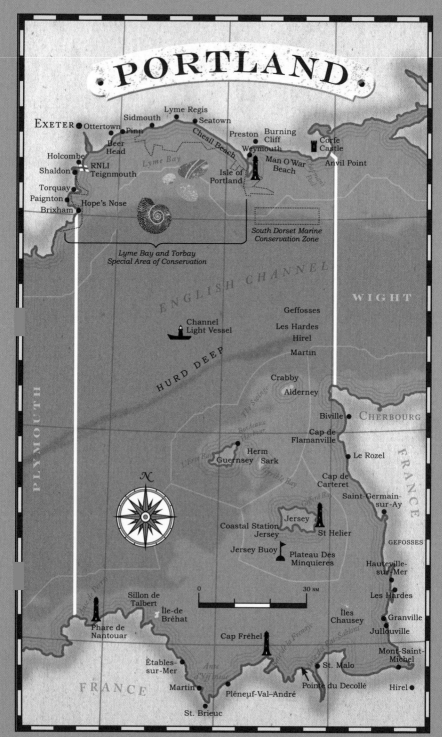

PORTLAND

Exeter • Ottertown
Sidmouth
Pinn
Lyme Regis
Seatown
Beer Head
Chesil Beach
Preston
Burning Cliff
Weymouth
Corfe Castle
Holcombe
RNLI Teignmouth
Lyme Bay
Man O'War Beach
Anvil Point
Shaldon
Isle of Portland
Torquay
Paignton
Brixham
Hope's Nose

South Dorset Marine Conservation Zone

Lyme Bay and Torbay
Special Area of Conservation

ENGLISH CHANNEL

WIGHT

Channel Light Vessel

Geffosses
Les Hardes
Hirel
Martin

HURD DEEP

Crabby
Alderney

PLYMOUTH

Biville
CHERBOURG

Cap de Flamanville

Herm
Guernsey Sark
Le Rozel

FRANCE

Cap de Carteret

Saint-Germain-sur-Ay

N

Jersey

Coastal Station
Jersey
St Helier

GEFOSSES

Jersey Buoy
Plateau Des Minquieres

Hauteville-sur-Mer

Sillon de Talbert
Île-de-Bréhat

Les Hardes

Îles Chausey

Granville
Jullouville

Phare de Nantouar

0   30 NM

Cap Fréhel
Mont-Saint-Michel

Étables-sur-Mer

St. Malo
Hirel

FRANCE
Martin
Pléneuf-Val–André
Pointe du Decollé

St. Brieuc

MAP 15

Difficulty
Fresh gale

Wind Southeast 5 or 6, becoming cyclonic 7 to 8 later
Sea state Slight or moderate, becoming rough later
Weather Rain then showers
Visibility Good, occasionally poor

START

1. Teeny village which shares its name with a big Lancashire city that has 1,000 times as many inhabitants

As you navigate your way along the coast, in a bay that was used for the 2012 Olympics, you will pass lagoons – some are natural; others here were created by quarrying enough stone to build St Paul's Cathedral. A note of caution. Portland is marked on the map as an island. On no account, though, try to sail between the island and the mainland, as they are connected by a barrier beach which protects the Bay from erosion, so arguably that word 'Isle' is deeply misleading.

2. Shingly site from which Ian McEwan stole some pebbles to keep on his desk while writing his novella about a honeymoon

You are about to sail over SM UB-74, a U-boat sunk by HMS *Lorna* in 1918, and HMS *M2*, a Royal Navy submarine monitor shipwrecked in 1932; the VHF channel for the harbour you are next approaching is 14, with working channel 16.

3. While we're being all literary, resort visited by Anne and Capt. Wentworth in *Persuasion* and by Meryl Streep for *The French Lieutenant's Woman*, on the 'mouth' of the 'river' 'Lim'

Slow down as you leave the bay: this is a rare chance to see minke whales and thresher sharks.

4. Cape that, fittingly, has three pubs within ten minutes' walk

On your starboard side is Teignmouth, setting-off point for Donald Crowhurst's ill-fated Teignmouth Electron.

5. Site of the Gleneagles Hotel, where John Cleese stayed in the early 1970s

Once you're past Channel Light Vessel, you're in the English Channel Traffic Separation Scheme. Think of a TSS like a bit of the sea where you 'drive on the right'. Awkwardly, though, you're crossing the main road. Just like with the Green Cross Code, go straight across at right angles. The first vessels you encounter will be coming from port side: try to pass them astern and if the lane is busy, delay your crossing.

You will soon need customs clearance, so have ready your forms and your yellow Q flag that announces 'my vessel is healthy and I require free pratique' (confusingly, Q used to mean just the opposite: that your ship is quarantined).

6. Where a bad navigator *trying* to get to 44°51'38.3"N 0°32'56.0"W might end up if they tapped on the wrong name in their navigation kit

Keep an eye out for snorkelers as you leave the harbour. Your next leg follows the same route as a one-hour ferry ride: beware of the sandstone ridge which emerges from the water as Les Casquets – the lighthouse flashes every 3.7 seconds.

You'll next be looking for a visitor mooring, marked by yellow buoys.

7. When you live on ____, you never have trouble trying to park

Your most direct route now will take you through three different economic zones. You will need to use cardinal marks to navigate around Chausey, geographically a Channel Island but politically French.

8. They *say* it's a big town, but it's only got the same population as, say, Chard

Hug the coast; you are passing Eisenhower's Supreme HQ base following D Day. You should probably know that you are entering an area with the greatest tidal range (15 metres) you will ever experience, unless you sail to Canada's Fundy Bay. Time your arrival and departure very carefully!

9. *Sometimes* it's an island and *sometimes* a pilgrim can walk there

If you're lucky, the sea will take on the colour that inspired the name 'Emerald Coast' as you approach your destination

10. Where, if you speak good enough French, you might encounter sea horses?

End

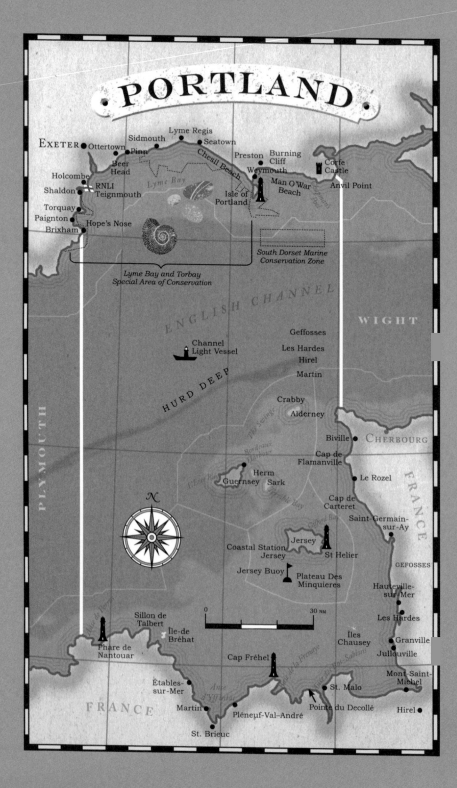

Difficulty
Light breeze

Wind Southwest 2 or 3
Sea state Moderate, occasionally
slight for a time
Weather Fair
Visibility Good

PORTLAND
VOYAGE 2

START

1. Sandy and pebbly location which shares its name with a spineless and poisonous Iberian

As the land disappears, you will feel for a moment as if you have Portland to yourself. This would be a mistake; you are about to enter a massive shipping lane. Pass to the stern of the monster ships. Try to get on the leading line half a mile before the harbour entrance, as it has a breakwater as protection against huge currents coming from the Swinge – thank the Victorian engineers.

2. Closest point to France where you can spend pounds

You are now in the Alderney Race, which is not a regatta. It's a strait with a current so strong that sailors here sometimes feel their boat is going forwards when it is actually in reverse.

3. This place, rather than the Isle of Wight, should use the name Cowes for its main town

Pass Coastal Station Jersey – which is run by the Jersey Met, not the UK Met Office – heading south.

4. Almost... jumbled up

End

The waves are moderate, taking
a pronounced long form and
creating many white horses.

PLYMOUTH

The Plymouth shipping area includes the southernmost point of mainland Britain, the inspiringly named Start Point. You share your own starting point with many through history, including the *Golden Hind* and the *Mayflower*, though you are staying firmly within the 468-nautical-mile perimeter of Plymouth.

There will be moments of quiet splendour: stretches of the south Cornwall landscapes are a World Heritage site, and you may later see basking sharks bobbing around enjoying a plankton lunch.

Towards the end, though, you will encounter the Mer d'Iroise. You might assume it is called that because it's a sea you can sail through to Ireland. Not a bit of it, Breton sailors will tell you. 'Iroise' means 'full of ire'; the coast is studded with search and rescue stations for good reason.

And let's take a moment to respect the River Plym: here we have a mighty port and a decent chunk of sea, each named for a waterway which is as long as the Thames gets wide.

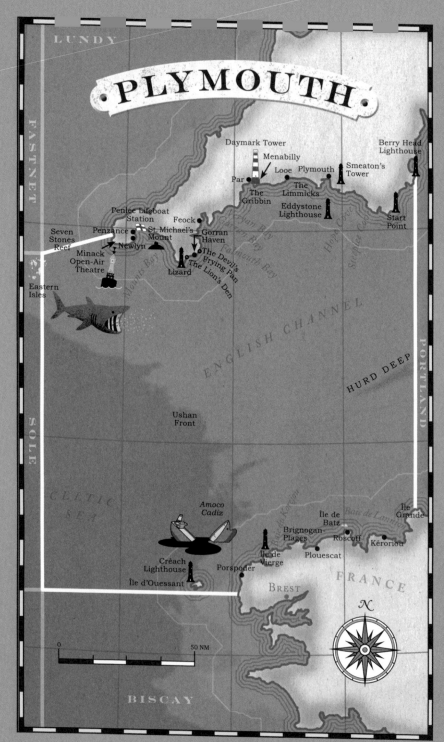

PLYMOUTH

LUNDY

FASTNET

SOLE

BISCAY

Daymark Tower

Menabilly

Par

Looe

Plymouth

Berry Head Lighthouse

Smeaton's Tower

The Gribbin

The Limmicks

Eddystone Lighthouse

Start Point

Penlee Lifeboat Station

Feock

Penzance

St. Michael's Mount

Gorran Haven

Seven Stones Reef

Newlyn

The Devil's Frying Pan

Minack Open-Air Theatre

Lizard

The Lion's Den

Eastern Isles

ENGLISH CHANNEL

Gerrans Bay

Veryan Bay

Falmouth Bay

Hope Cove

Start Bay

HURD DEEP

PORTLAND

Ushan Front

Mount's Bay

CELTIC SEA

Amoco Cadiz

Île de Batz

Île Grande

Baie de Lannion

Brignogan-Plages

Roscoff

Kéroriou

Créach Lighthouse

Île d'Ouessant

Porspoder

Île de Vierge

Plouescat

FRANCE

BREST

N

MAP 16

Difficulty
Strong breeze

Wind West backing southwest, 5 to 7
Sea state Moderate, occasionally rough
Weather Rain later
Visibility Good

START

1. Where historians are now sure a game was *not* interrupted

To the south of your leg is the first offshore lighthouse, the awesome Eddystone: during the initial construction, a privateer kidnapped the builders and took them to France, but did not get the reaction he'd hoped for. Louis XIV had the privateer locked in the Bastille and the men returned to Cornwall with the note: 'I am at war with the English, not with humanity.'

2. There's a public one here in the Millpool car park and another on Marine Drive...

Beware the Ranneys (reef) and the Limmicks (rocks) as you leave; as you sail past Polperro, you're crossing the site of a submerged forest, which became a fossil-y destination for Victorian tourists.

3. ... *and* appropriately, there are four golf courses within a couple of miles of *here*

Two points of interest: the striped tower on the cliffs ended years of tragic confusion between the headland you're passing and the one you're about to pass; and the grand house nearby was once home to Daphne du Maurier and the inspiration for *Rebecca*'s Manderley estate.

4. Where you can get a hell of a full English?

Next, you'll pass by a blowhole created when the roof of a sea cave collapsed in 1847; when the weather intensifies, people gather around it to watch the sea appearing to actually boil.

5. What a komodo dragon really is

If you're passing at night and think you see shipwrecking going on, don't be alarmed: it's most likely just Aidan Turner and the lads filming some more scenes for *Poldark*.

6. Gets on a reddish-brown horse?

Another submerged forest reveals how far the sea level has risen; in fact, the great tor that pokes out of the sea – the one that you're headed for – was once part of the mainland.

7. Pilgrimage part of whose name appeared on Marks and Spencer pants for 70 years

The harbour lights you're approaching can be difficult to distinguish from the shore lights, so be wary, especially in south or southeasterly winds.

8. Where, in 1879, some buccaneers released the daughters of an incredibly up-to-date – and musical – senior military officer

An Ordnance Survey tidal observatory was set up here in 1915, taking hourly readings, by watching two floats connected by chains; whenever we talk about anything having a 'height above sea level', it's the average sea level right here that we're talking about!

9. Where you can see *The Tempest* in a tempest

The top of the Runnel Stone reef was knocked off by SS *City of Westminster* in 1923, since when it has stopped causing shipwrecks; use it as your starting point and leave two hours before High Water Dover.

10. Not on *this* map, they're not

Check your paperwork is in order before you leave UK waters; also, you're approaching what they say is the world's largest diveable wreck.

11. Where a clumsy navigator aiming for 18°5'37"N 64°49'49"W might end up

Approach your destination from the channel with the mainland, but only at half-tide or higher.

12. Where you might look for pipistrellez or flying foxez?

End

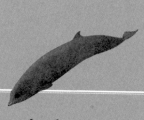

*The sea tends to heap up; as the waves
break, streaks of white foam show
you the direction of the wind.*

· BISCAY ·

The waves that arrive here from the Americas have often spent their journey getting bigger and bigger. Then you've got a colossal amount of wind, including those trade winds headed for the doldrums – a gale can make those waves steeper still.

And then you've got depressions, also arriving from the west, which dry out and appear here in the form of thunderstorms. The warmer waters mean things can get pretty violent pretty fast.

Put these together and you've got a good idea, when you hear Mary's refrain from the old ballad...

> *For seven years, I've been constantly waiting*
> *Since he crossed the Bay of Biscay–o.*

... whether or not her William is coming back to shore.

And you have *two* voyages to make here. However, as you'll see from the forecasts below, the conditions are in fact pretty favourable.

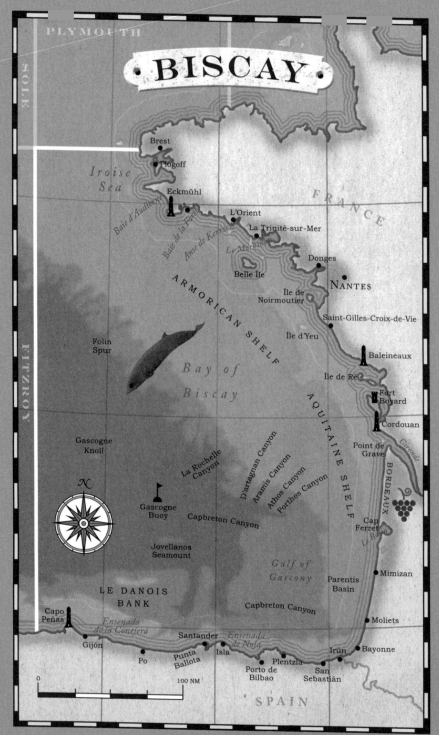

MAP 17

Difficulty	
Fresh breeze	

Wind Northwest 5, backing west 6 to 7 later
Sea state Moderate, occasionally rough
Weather Fair
Visibility Good

BISCAY
VOYAGE 1

START

1. **Start**: A Manchester restaurant accidentally served a £4,500 one in 2019

You are leaving one of *seven* terminals, so pay attention!

2. **Castle which gave its name – and location – to a game show from 1990 to 2016**

They took defensive structures pretty seriously here for a long time.

3. **The other three eventually let him join**

All manner of little sports vessels may be jiggering about.

4. **Three men in a boat?**

NB: 'zone des exercices de tir' means 'shooting practice'.

5. **Ravine named after a city named after a rock**

End

Difficulty
Moderate gale

Wind Northwest, 7 to 8
Sea state Rough, occasionally high later in west
Weather Squally showers
Visibility Good occasionally poor

START

1. Where your *amie* might be a bosom buddy?

You approach the ocean through a steep-sided bottleneck; be patient.

2. She's the smallest one, and red

Your destination has been a port as long as there have been ports.

3. It announced the closure of 140 branches in 2019

It's illegal to take cats on to the island on your port side.

4. But, I mean, it's blatantly part of the mainland

You can discuss the many sandbanks with the marinas on VHF channel 9.

5. It's just a three-hour walk to the Guggenheim

… and as you leave the coast, you are just staying in the same nation's waters.

6. Radcliffe's terse job description

End

· TRAFALGAR ·

This is not like pootling about on the familiar coastline of the UK. Trafalgar is, of course, the name of a bay (from the Arabic طرف الغرب, 'Cape in the West') which gave its name to the battle where Nelson sank Napoleon's ambitions to invade the British Isles but did not live to see the end of the engagement. Don't get distracted looking for Trafalgar the bay or Trafalgar the site of the battle, as they are *just* outside Trafalgar the shipping area.

Also just outside this area is a continent which does not feature in any of our voyages, though your fellow voyagers may be heading *to* and *from* Casablanca or other African spots. Had you been here 500 years ago, your fellow voyagers would have been part of the Age of Discovery, stealing silver and snaffling spices.

Nowadays, you share the waters with other kinds of vehicle: when you're near the coast, you must avoid operating areas for the seaplanes, used to draw water to fight forest fires further in to the Portuguese mainland.

There will be significant currents at times, though you may be more struck by the surface drift as the sea's surface is carried along by prevailing winds.

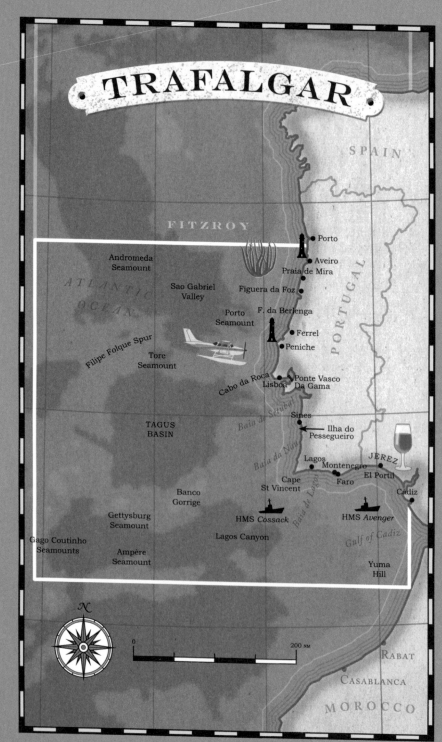

TRAFALGAR

SPAIN

FITZROY

Andromeda
Seamount

ATLANTIC
OCEAN

Sao Gabriel
Valley

Porto
Seamount

F. da Berlenga

Filipe Folque Spur

Tore
Seamount

Cabo da Roca

TAGUS
BASIN

Baía de Setúbal

Baía da Nau

Banco
Gorrige

Gettysburg
Seamount

Gago Coutinho
Seamounts

Ampère
Seamount

Lagos Canyon

Porto

Aveiro

Praia de Mira

Figuera da Foz

Ferrel

Peniche

Ponte Vasco
Da Gama

Lisboa

PORTUGAL

Sines

Ilha do
Pessegueiro

Lagos

Montenegro

Cape
St Vincent

Faro

El Portil

JEREZ

Cadiz

HMS *Cossack*

Baía de Lagos

HMS *Avenger*

Gulf of Cadiz

Yuma
Hill

N

0   200 NM

RABAT

CASABLANCA

MOROCCO

MAP 18

Difficulty
Moderate gale

Wind West veering northwest, 5 to 6,
becoming variable 8 later
Sea state Rough in northeast
Weather Showers
Visibility Moderate to poor

TRAFALGAR
VOYAGE 1

START

1. Manzanilla, Amontillado, Oloroso... they all come from (and get their name from) here

There are extensive shoals as you leave the bay; keep one and a half nautical miles seaward of them, then have your paperwork ready, as you'll be entering a different country's waters.

2. Regal-sounding card game which Nicholas Rostov plays in *War and Peace*, losing a cool 43,000 roubles

The coastal dunes provide plenty of shelter, but navigation should not be attempted in strong southerlies, even for the next short hop.

3. Once part of the Kingdom of Serbs, Croats and Slovenes

In your next port, you hand your documentation to the marina staff, who will distribute it to the local authorities.

4. Fifteenth-century slave traders coming from Nigeria sailed in to here from a city with the same name

You'll now pass over a canyon of the same name, and round a cape which gave its name to a famous battle of 1797. And to another in 1780. Oh, and it gave its name to a few other battles as well: 1337, 1606, 1641, 1681, 1693, 1719, 1751, and 1833, to be precise.

5. Might mathematical sailors approach this port
at tangents?

Do not leave your boat unattended, as southerly gales often bring
quite the swell to this marina.

6. He was the first to link, with an ocean route,
Asia and Europe

For geological reasons, there are some magnetic anomalies around
here which can put your navigation out by five degrees more or
three degrees less!

7. It rhymes with the capital of Queensland

And the shoals on the bank of the river you're in are prone to
breaking in poor weather. This journey will get simpler soon, though.

8. Californian location for wine-road-movie *Sideways*

OK, pay attention. See those two islands you're approaching?
The one which has a square tower is actually a peninsula, so do
go between them. And then keep at least five cables between you
and the Cabo Raso.

9. (And staying with American cinema) Wil, star
of *Downhil?*

End

Difficulty
Moderate breeze

Wind Northwest, 4
Sea state Mainly slight
Weather Good
Visibility Good

TRAFALGAR
VOYAGE 2

START

1. It would be fitting if you navigated by the stars from here

You're about to leave international waters, though it will be a long time before you have sight of land, let alone a port requiring documentation.

2. It was discovered in 1858, which is a lot longer than four-score-and-seven years ago

Not to alarm you, but the Portuguese authorities are very interested in boats in this area and you may be asked random questions, such as the horsepower of your engine: they're on the lookout for contraband.

Now you're sailing over a geological fault known as the Azores–Gibraltar Transform Fault, and the epicentre of the notorious 1755 Lisbon earthquake, which sent tsunamis to Cornwall, to Galway and even to Barbados.

3. And *this* is a fitting place to measure the strength of the current

End

FITZROY

This is the only area named for a person. Until 2002, it was known as Finisterre. But Finisterre is an international name which means 'the end of the land' – and what the speakers of one language consider the edge of the world may not tally with what the speakers of another think.

This kind of ambiguity could be fatal at sea. And so, in 2002, Spanish meteorologists – whose Finisterre went further along the Portuguese coast – asked the Met Office to come up with a new name.

That this often perilous area should be named after the pioneering meteorologist we met in the introduction is multiply cheering.

Most cheeringly, it rights a wrong. Bob FitzRoy was insufficiently hailed in his lifetime. He managed to counter a puritanical Victorian distaste for prognostication by coining the phrase 'weather forecast', but he was considered a massive irritant by the powerful owners of ships.

If FitzRoy forecast a storm, captains knew there would likely *be* a storm and stayed in harbour, infuriating the shipping magnates, for whom a ship sinking with its cargo – and crew – was at least covered by insurance.

A ship waiting in dock for safe conditions, by contrast, makes nobody rich.

They tried to have the Shipping Forecast banned and, following FitzRoy's untimely death, successfully lobbied parliament to have the warnings withdrawn. Happily, the combined forces of the Met Office, sailors and the British public got it back.

And so now, thanks to meteorology, mariners in FitzRoy know to bear in mind the way the gulf stream splits, giving a half-knot southerly drift, often combined with those northeasterlies that run along the Portuguese coast. They also share their waters with some of the biggest oysters you'll ever see.

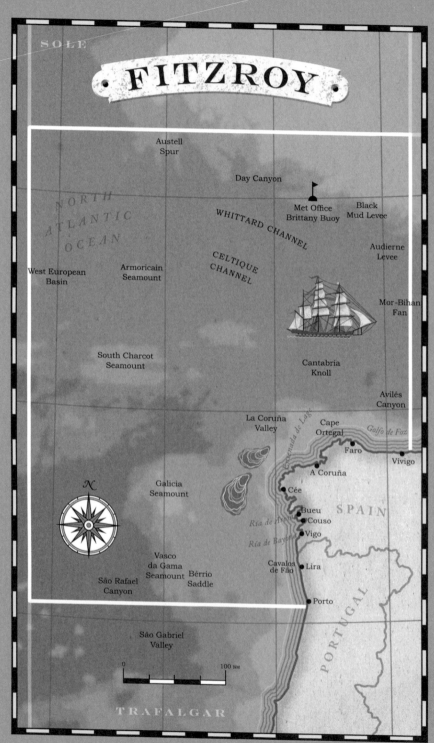

SOLE

FITZROY

Austell
Spur

Day Canyon

NORTH
ATLANTIC
OCEAN

WHITTARD CHANNEL

Met Office
Brittany Buoy

Black
Mud Levee

Audierne
Levee

CELTIQUE
CHANNEL

West European
Basin

Armoricain
Seamount

Mor-Bihan
Fan

South Charcot
Seamount

Cantabria
Knoll

Avilés
Canyon

La Coruña
Valley

Ensenada de Lage

Cape
Ortegal

Golfo de Foz

Faro

Vívigo

A Coruña

Cée

Galicia
Seamount

Bueu

SPAIN

Couso

Ría de Arosa

Vigo

Ría de Bayona

Vasco
da Gama
Seamount

Bérrio
Saddle

Cavalos
de Fão

Lira

São Rafael
Canyon

Porto

PORTUGAL

São Gabriel
Valley

0   100 KM

TRAFALGAR

MAP 19

Wind Southwesterly veering westerly
6 to gale 8, perhaps severe gale 9 later
Sea state Rough becoming high later
in northwest
Weather Thundery showers
Visibility Moderate or good,
occasionally poor

START

1.

That great gulf you're sailing away from was named after a
brilliant British geophysicist called Geoffrey...

2. Where, appropriately enough, tea clippers used to sail

... and appropriately, you're at the outer portion of the
Shamrock Channel.

3. A name which presents, in one word, the Auld Alliance?

For you, what you're passing is a canyon; for the sea's permanent
inhabitants, in search of some organic matter, it's kind of a larder.

4. It bordered – and merged with – León

And your endpoint here is named after one of the ships used
by Vasco da Gama on his first attempt to reach the Cape of
Good Hope.

5. Gabriel: 'God is my strength'; Michael: 'Who is like God?'; ____: 'It is God who heals'

End

SOLE

You might have sometimes wondered: how do forecasters know what's going to happen? The answer is that weather systems (that is, areas of hot and of cold air) generally move from west to east, so it's possible to tell when a front (where warm and cool air collide) is coming.

So, with an area of low pressure, forecasters know the ballet that will be played out between the warm and cold air: when the heavy rain turns to showers, when the wispy cirrus clouds will thicken up, and so on.

And we know that weather systems arriving *here*, thanks to the gulf stream, bless these waters with more welcoming warmth than you find on the other side of the Shipping Areas.

Welcoming, that is, to fish. Like, say, sole – although it was the French who originally named the Banc de la Grande Sole seamount that gives our Shipping Area its name, and they confusingly say that it wasn't to do with fish.

Sole might be around 110km² of sea, but the only land is that balmy 16km² collection of islands just tucked into the northeast corner... so don't expect a lot of facilities on this journey.

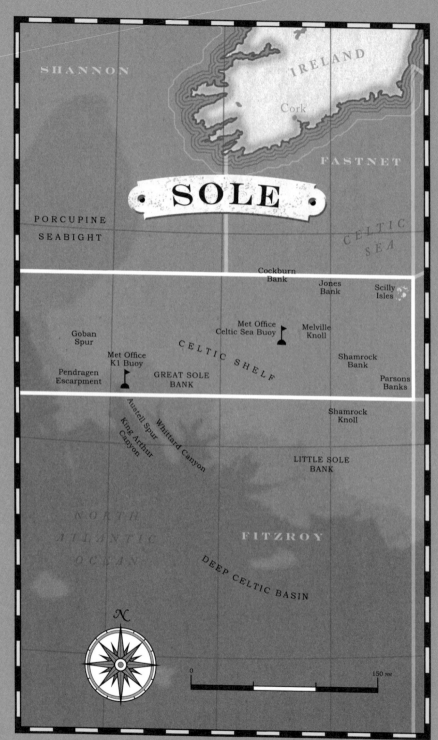

MAP 20

Difficulty
Fresh gale

Wind Southwesterly, veering
northwesterly for a time, 6 to gale 8
Sea state Mainly slight
Weather Squally showers
Visibility Good, occasionally poor

START

1. Britten used him for an opera

At first tack north-northeast of a straight line to the next point,
later north-northwest...

2. No mariner wants to see this cupboard

... start west-northwest of a straight line, later west-southwest...

3. They sound ridiculous

... start south-southeast of a straight line, later south-southwest...

4. 1: Cook...; 4: Clark...; 7: Shipman...; 10: ____

... start west-southwest of a straight line, later west-northwest...

5. Name given to five yachts by Sir Thomas Lipton, son of Fermanagh smallholders who became a famous tea baron

... start north-northwest of a straight line, later north-northeast.

6. *Also*, his best known character was played by Gregory Peck

End

LUNDY

Ah, you may be thinking. This looks reassuringly familiar. The Gower peninsula. Those Celtic landmarks along the coasts of an area that connects the Cornish and the Welsh to the Irish (technically, 116 metres of the coast at Kilmuckridge are part of the Lundy Shipping Area).

Think again.

The Bristol Channel has the world's second-largest tidal range and, given that you won't be visiting Canada's Bay of Fundy, the largest *you'll* be experiencing, so watch out for hidden sandbanks. It's also extremely busy and the rough waves can reach 4 metres. At least your visibility is fair.

Here's just one of Lundy's grisly tales. In 1801, the two-man team at Smalls Lighthouse, just near the puffin-inhabited Lundy itself, was halved in size when one took ill and no help arrived. His colleague assembled a makeshift coffin and arranged a burial at sea, but the casket split open and the wind made the body's arm look as if it was beckoning the survivor to join the watery grave. He, of course, went insane, and from then on lighthouse teams had a minimum of three men.

And here's a typical local ditty: 'From Padstow Bar to Lundy Light / Is a sailor's grave, by day or night'. Let's hope the old Welsh sea god St Dewi smiles on *your* journey.

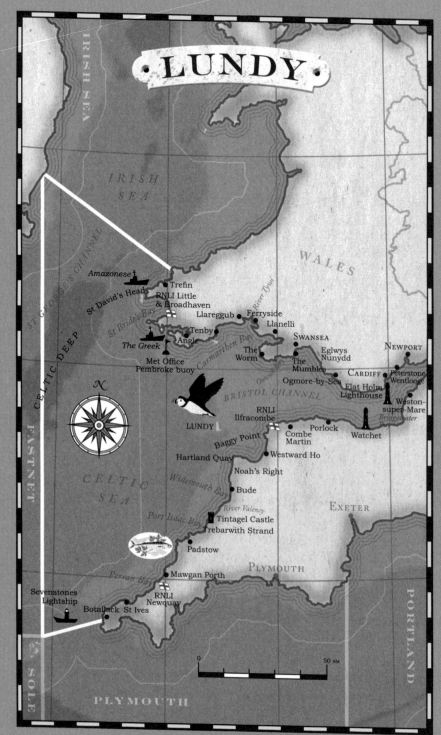

LUNDY

IRISH SEA

WALES

IRISH SEA

Amazonese

Trefin
RNLI Little
& Broadhaven
Llareggub
Ferryside
Llanelli
SWANSEA

St David's Head
St Bride's Bay
Tenby
Angle

The Greek
Met Office
Pembroke buoy

The
Worm
The
Mumbles
Eglwys
Nunydd

NEWPORT

Carmarthen Bay

Oxwich Bay

Ogmore-by-Sea

CARDIFF
Flat Holm
Lighthouse

Peterstone
Wentlooge

Weston-
super-Mare

N

BRISTOL CHANNEL

CELTIC DEEP

LUNDY

RNLI
Ilfracombe

Porlock

Watchet

Bridgewater

FASTNET

Baggy Point

Combe
Martin

Hartland Quay

Westward Ho

CELTIC
SEA

Noah's Right

Widemouth Bay

Bude

EXETER

Port Isaac Bay

River Valency

Tintagel Castle
Trebarwith Strand

PLYMOUTH

Padstow

Perran Bay

Mawgan Porth

PORTLAND

Sevenstones
Lightship

Botallack   St Ives

RNLI
Newquay

SOLE

0   50 NM

PLYMOUTH

MAP 21

Difficulty
Fresh breeze

Wind Southwest 4 or 5, backing
southeast, veering south
Sea state Moderate or rough
Weather Rain
Visibility Fair

START

1. Destination in an encounter in which the narrator witnesses cruelty to 2,744 felines

The view from here inspired Virginia Woolf to write *To the Lighthouse*, though you're right in thinking that the novel itself is set in the Hebrides Shipping Area.

2. Town sometimes referred to, not *especially* fondly, as Padstein

If you arrive here too late and find the gate of the inner harbour is closed, you're allowed to moor in The Pool.

3. GCHQ's westernmost UK eavesdropping station (Google it if you're brave enough)

The quay over on starboard side used to be a harbour but is no longer (for good reason) and has an impressive shipwreck museum (also for good reason).

4. Part of the map that *should* have an exclamation mark but just *doesn't*

This is a part of the coast where mariners really do not want for harbours and anchorages.

5. Good place, when it's early, to find a bird?

As you pass Flat Holm Island, think of its curious mixture of past inhabitants from Vikings taking a rest, through silver-miners, smugglers and lighthouse-keepers, to cholera patients in quarantine; nowadays, you can see blue slowworms.

6. Town whose hyphenated name literally means 'Town in the West That's on the Sea' (think about it...)

On port side are the Quantock Hills, whose sea views inspired Coleridge to think of an Ancient Mariner while walking with the Wordsworths; less poetical is the name of the nearby nudist beach, Wild Pear.

7. ... hmm, well it's part of the bay at Swans... er, not just that... it's, uh, a bunch of villag... er, it's on the Gower Peninsu-thing...

These waters are unusually prone to unpleasant non-native species, such as the Clawed Frog (imported in the 1950s to provide pregnancy tests for humans, they escaped from their lab) and the Killer Shrimp, which massacres regular shrimp.

8. Only town marked on the map whose name has one letter of the English alphabet appearing as often as all the others put together

A pirate yacht was seized here with £60m of narcotics in 2019.

9. Right ____

End

FASTNET

There's a reason the biennial Fastnet Race is known as one the toughest yachting competitions. Out here, by the edge of enormity, the weather is unpredictable, though you can probably expect a *lot* of grey at the beginning of *your* voyage.

Later, though, you will get cosily familiar with the south coast of Ireland, which is a friend you should stick close to. Lights and landmarks are there to keep you from joining the many sunken crafts you will be sailing over. On the corner is the Fastnet Rock itself, a Norse name meaning 'Sharp-Toothed Islet' and more fondly called 'Ireland's Teardrop', weepily tipping a captain's hat to countless emigrants hoping to reach the Americas.

The mighty Atlantic tide splits somewhere south of the Skelligs Islands, half of it going clockwise around the island of Ireland and the other anti-clockwise. Where they reunite, in Liverpool Bay, the effect is immense. You need only be aware of it when you're closest to Wales.

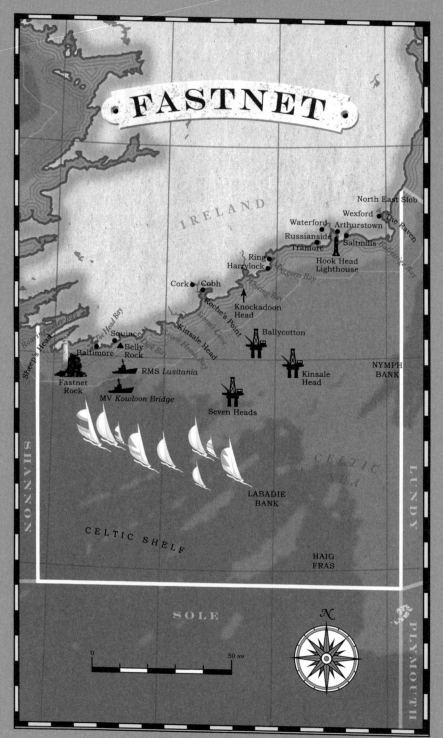

FASTNET

North East Slob

Wexford
The Raven

Waterford
Arthurstown

IRELAND

Russianside
Saltmills

Tramore

Ring
Hook Head
Lighthouse

Harrylock

Cork • Cobh

Roche's Point

Knockadoon
Head

Sheep's Head

Squince

Ballycotton

Baltimore

Belly
Rock

Kinsale Head

NYMPH
BANK

RMS *Lusitania*

Fastnet
Rock

Kinsale
Head

MV *Kowloon Bridge*

Seven Heads

CELTIC
SEA

LUNDY

LABADIE
BANK

SHANNON

CELTIC SHELF

HAIG
FRAS

SOLE

N

PLYMOUTH

0   50 NM

MAP 22

Difficulty
Fresh gale

Wind Southeast becoming cyclonic,
6 to 7, occasionally gale 8
Sea state Moderate or rough
Weather Showers
Visibility Moderate, occasionally poor

START

1. Where the 1967 European Cup sits

There are fewer natural resources here for mankind to grab than in other shipping areas, but away off on the starboard side is the Kinsale Head gas field, which supplied a lot of power to Ireland at the end of the twentieth century (and is now nearly all gone).

2. Spot *also* indicated by the coordinates 22°17'38.0"N 114°10'53.9"E, in a way

... there's a grim connection between that destination and this one...

3. It was actually 700 days later that Wilson waged war

Expect westerly winds, but also expect a bunch of low-pressure systems to create a weather pattern that never stays still.

4. Where a dryad makes a deposit, or an oread gets an overdraft?

Get your tricolour flag ready: you are approaching land for the first time this journey. The harbour is guarded by three banks which have a tendency to – there's no easy way of telling you this – move around...

5. Poe poem

... and while you're in the area...

6. Sloven from Sunderland

... and they'll have moved again by the time you leave port. The water you'll go through next is so reefy that an islander in the nineteenth century built a special hut 'in which he placed stores of potatoes, whiskey, wood, candles, and matches, in case of any shipwrecked people arriving there at night'.

7. Place with a lot of NaCl history

Allow the world's oldest operational lighthouse to guide you past the limestone and red sandstone.

8. Camelot?

This is a tiny leg, but you will cross a county boundary in the water.

9. What *Pravda* provided during the Cold War

As you pass Tramore, you will be guided by three pillars erected in 1823 by Lloyds of London, on top of the middle of which is the 3-metre 'Metal Man' who, the locals say, calls out 'Keep off, keep off / Good ship from me / For I am the rock / Of misery'; listen to the Metal Man.

10. Port blockage

You're passing another port which has some grisly tourist appeal as it turned out to be, rather than New York, the final port of call of RMS *Titanic.*

11. In modern parlance, it's a facial expression that combines a wince with a squint

The harbour here is protected from the prevailing southwesterlies, but do look out for Belly Rock, which the unwary are unaware of until upon it.

12. *Not* the Maryland port whose harbour was the setting for season two of *The Wire*

Rocky shoals break the current here and, unless it's a strong southerly, you'll be out of the wind.

13. A garfish, swimming, might be seen here?

End

*The waves are very high with long
over-hanging crests. The tumbling
of the sea, now white across the surface,
is becoming heavy and shock-like.*

IRISH SEA

This is the only shipping area with all the nations of the British Isles, so you'll be encountering, among others, Irish ports with Nordic names (Wicklow is, they say, a Viking name meaning 'Meadow of the Vikings', which smacks of gloating), English castles on the Welsh coastline and English cities built by the Irish.

The North Atlantic is at both ends of the Irish Sea but, in between, you're sharing sheltered waters with tentacled sea gooseberries and lion's mane jellyfish, which use their stingers to pull in fish and which are in turn devoured by the leatherback turtles which hang around here specifically for their delicious jellyfish suppers.

The Irish Sea typically offers calmer waters and better visibility than the areas it abuts, but, as you are about to find out, navigation on some routes can still be quite the challenge.

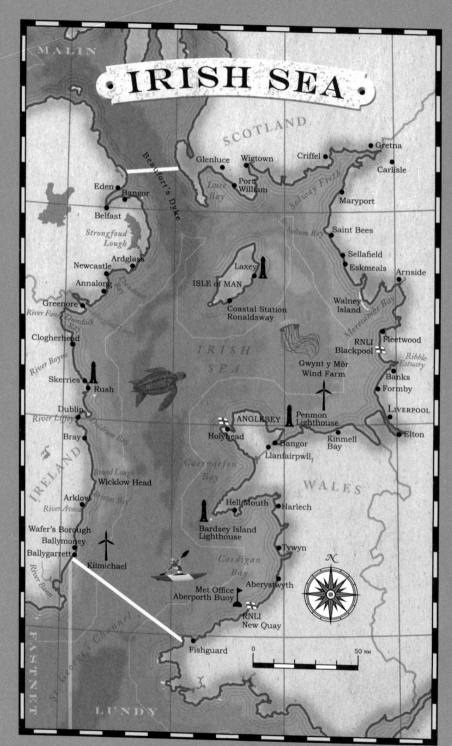

MAP 23

Difficulty
Whole gale

Wind East, veering southeast,
gale 8 to storm 10, imminent
Sea state Moderate, occasionally smooth
Weather Rain or thundery showers
Visibility Moderate

START

1. Instruction given to various goons in the *Godfather* movies

There's safe passage between the offshore shallow banks and you can get up a decent speed if you've planned well for this leg...

2. Career

... and there's often an unpleasant swell in the final bay of this leg.

3. River whose name appears in UK calendars, not meaning a *great* deal to some of those on *one* side of this stretch of water

It's time now to pass by the British Isles' largest sea inlet, the autumn landing point for thousands of Brent geese, freshly arrived from the Arctic.

4. Site of a £101m tourist attraction about an unsuccessful journey

Now is one of your best chances of spotting basking sharks; to the port, Luce Bay, as you'd expect from the name, is the source of the greatest beauty you'll see in any of your voyages.

5. **It's called that because it's where the Devil apparently dropped a lobster pot, to use its technical name**

You'll pass some islands where four-fifths of the sandy and marshy coasts have been transformed for leisure or farming in the last century...

6. **To canonise workers and their queen?**

... but not at Eskmeals, making it one of the last places the natterjack toad can feel safe to come and emit its booming, grunting mating calls. Maybe pull anchor for a while and listen to these strange striped beasts? No offence taken if you don't.

7. **Its name changed, for obvious reasons, in 1981**

Listen up, quite literally: the way the tidal bay narrows suddenly, combined with an already massive tidal range, means that the water rises very suddenly around here; the siren gives eight sounds 2.25 and 1.75h before and after high tide.

8. **E. ____ said that...**

(... tip your cap as you pass, for on your port side is the port where a pharmacist dreamed up the Fisherman's Friend lozenge...)

9. **... his childhood hero was G. ____, 'another native of Lancashire. I would certainly like to follow in his footsteps'**

If you think you can espy 100 giant iron men staring out to sea, you do not have cabin fever. This is Antony Gormley's installation

'Another Place'. In fact, if you don't see 100 giant iron men, it really is time for a rest. And don't get distracted and have an accident, as the local coastguards were worried that Gormley's intervention would make this happen.

10. Town whose name, if written in full, would be 152 miles long on this map

You're passing by spots popular among thornback skate, at least as long as they don't get caught accidentally in trawling nets due to their notoriously thorny backs.

11. Didn't we have a lovely time the day we went to the setting for the opening of Act 3 of *Henry IV, Part 1*?

Eighteenth-century traders were supposed to pay one penny per ship as a levy to maintain the lighthouse you're passing, but so many avoided it that its founder died a ruined man.

12. ... but I thought we *just*...

Castles like the one you'll pass were built on the shoreline by the English because, they say, trying to get materials across the land was too often stymied by Welsh ambush.

13. What Pauline Fowler and Kurt Cobain had in common

End

There are small waves, but they are becoming longer with white horses fairly frequent.

· SHANNON ·

Your adventures in the other areas involving stretches of the Irish coastline involve more fancy marinas that please the fancy mariner; along the southern end of the west coast, you're communing with the Atlantic proper.

Eight centuries ago, your voyage would surely have included a hopeful stopover at Hy-Brasil, an alluring circular island divided down its middle by a strait, known then for its rabbit inhabitants and persistent mist and known now for having been named Brasil before Brazil and for, like Atlantis, having altogether fallen off reputable maps.

They were right, of course: there really *is* land to be found if you keep going; it's just a couple of thousand, not a couple of hundred miles away. And, as we'll see, you can make it there in a banana-shaped boat made of animal hides. You'll be glad to hear that you're staying within the boundaries of the shipping area fed by rivers including the British Isles' longest, the Shannon.

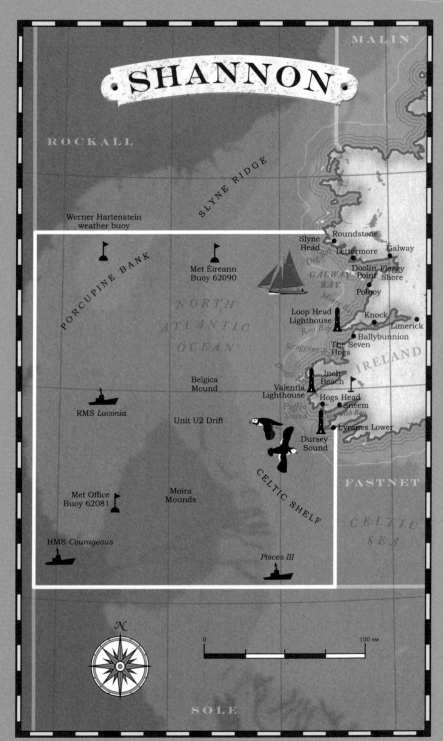

SHANNON

MALIN

ROCKALL

SLYNE RIDGE

Werner Hartenstein
weather buoy

Slyne
Head   Roundstone

Met Éireann   Lettermore   Galway
Buoy 62090   PORCUPINE BANK   Doolin Fleggy
                                  Point   Shore
                        GALWAY
                        BAY
                        Polgoy

NORTH
ATLANTIC   Loop Head   Knock
OCEAN   Lighthouse   Limerick
                        Ballybunnion
                The Seven   IRELAND
                Hogs

                        Inch
Belgica   Beach
Mound   Valentia
              Lighthouse   Hogs Head
RMS Laconia   Sneem
              Unit U2 Drift   Lyranes Lower

                        Dursey
                        Sound   FASTNET

                                CELTIC SHELF

Met Office   Moira   CELTIC
Buoy 62081   Mounds   SEA

HMS Courageous

                        Pisces III

N

0   100 NM

SOLE

MAP 24

Difficulty
Gentle breeze

Wind Northwest, backing southwest
for a time, 3 or 4, occasionally 6 later
Sea state Moderate, occasionally rough
Weather Occasional rain
Visibility Good

START

1. 'A large nose is in fact the sign of an affable man, good, courteous, witty, liberal, ____, such as I am' (*Cyrano de Bergerac*)

These waters have long been home to trawlers and drift nets.

2. Not to be confused with The Needles

The off-lying islands do provide some shelter but southwesterlies and indeed westerlies still make it to where you'll be hoping to anchor.

3. Sea lough commemorated in song (in song) by the NYPD Choir

The shore you're heading for was described (in prose) by Seamus Heaney as a 'glorious exultation of air and sea and swans'.

4. You'd be disappointed if you didn't see a tricolour as you approached

The currents here can depend on how much of the recent Munster rain has been deposited around you by the river's outflow.

5. Its paper is known as the *Post* / King's Island, they say, has a ghost / Frank McCourt wrote in his / Dour memoirs like '*Tis* / Of this port that's tucked in from the coast

The duration of rise and fall can be pretty much even in this estuary.

6. Word that can precede 'up', 'down', 'in', 'out', 'about'... and, more distinctively, 'kneed'

Keep an eye out for semi-competent snorkelling students as you approach.

7. Fourth sequel to a story about the wisdom of choosing appropriate building materials?

Keep an eye out for semi-competent surfing students as you approach.

8. Nonsense: its sand covers over three nautical miles!

They say the sixth-century St Brendan reached the Americas from here in a leather boat; in 1976 an explorer proved it could be done.

9. Interestingly, it's often *rwwwwwwww rwwwwwwww*, a lot like a chainsaw

European storm-petrels, here, and Manx shearwaters.

10. It shares a name with an inn in the *Harry Potter* universe

There is a five-fathom curve of coastal danger here.

11. Are you approaching The Edge of Irish waters...?

You're pretty much following the tread of a sinuous underwater stair.

12. ⚓ ⚓ ⚓

End

·ROCKALL·

The Scottish civil parish of Harris (pop.: 1,916) is bigger than you might think. The island itself is about 26 miles wide from east to west, but the parish continues west for another 230-odd miles... to include the desolate dot in the sea known as Rockall.

In 1955, at the tail end of the contraction of the British Empire, came one final spurt of expansion. HMS *Vidal* (named after Vice-Admiral A.T.E. Vidal, who had been the first to chart Rockall, in 1851) sent a helicopter over the rock. Four marines were winched down carrying a mast and a UK flag.

As our journeys keep reminding us, it's not the land that's important here. Only those who enjoy trying to survive in horrible environments have spent any time on wretched Rockall. It's handy to be able to claim the airspace above it, and more importantly, the right to go looking for fish and fuel around it.

There is plenty to look for. Previously unspotted creatures – of the clam / worm / snail varieties – have been found where you'll be sailing. But all that life is under the water. The Rockall Area also includes the most picturesque part of Ireland: but *your* journey may take you nowhere near Belmullet.

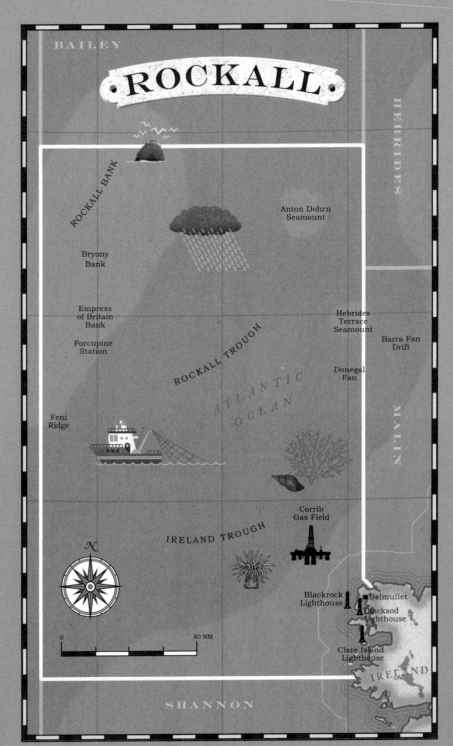

MAP 25

Difficulty
Strong breeze

Wind South, veering west or
southwest 5 to 6
Sea state Moderate, becoming rough
Weather Rain or drizzle, then
showers later
Visibility Moderate or poor,
occasionally good later

START

1. Railway terminus where there is never a points failure?

If you do encounter another boat around here, have your affairs
in order, as it may well be one of various countries' naval or
fisheries-patrol vessels...

2. One place you *don't* expect to find this garden pest!

... although you may also see a demersal trawler: a boat full of
scientists whose field of interest is not where you are, or the ocean
floor, but the area just above the ocean floor...

**3. The *only* feature in this Shipping Area named after
a prodigiously bearded Prussian**

... and any marine biologist would be thrilled to be where you are
now – on top of an area of extraordinary biodiversity: there's
cold-water coral down there and it supports all kinds of creatures.

**4. One who might watch every play in a Brian Friel
festival?**

... and if the word 'biodiversity' instantly makes you think:
'fossil fuels-to-be', you're not alone...

5. From which to watch Lewis & Harris FA games?

... finally, a reminder that other vessels may simply be blithely passing through.

6. She was probably carrying gold

End

MALIN

Even if this is your first time in the Malin shipping area, you may know it by osmosis. If you were shown a picture of Staffa's *Fingal's Cave,* you'd know it, and you also perhaps know it through the concert music it's provoked; if your tastes are happily more pop, there is, as you'll see, a peninsula further south which inspired quite a famous Christmas number one. There is no musical escape.

Around these parts is Jura, where George Orwell took some quiet time to write *Nineteen Eighty-Four,* and across the water you can see the area around Sligo immortalised time and again by W.B. Yeats. In short, these are coasts that have long inspired many – and in between are waters with jaw-dropping history: it was off Antrim's Lacada Point that divers discovered, in 2017, the Spanish Armada's galleass *Girona,* replete with its sixteenth-century gold.

There's even a monster in Loch Morar, though it's admittedly a much less lucrative beast than Nessie and – unless some very unexpected southerlies appear – you're no' going that way.

And with perhaps less fanfare, part of Malin has been named as the UK's hardest-to-pronounce place name: Ballachulish Bay (simple, though, right? *ba-la-HOOlish*).

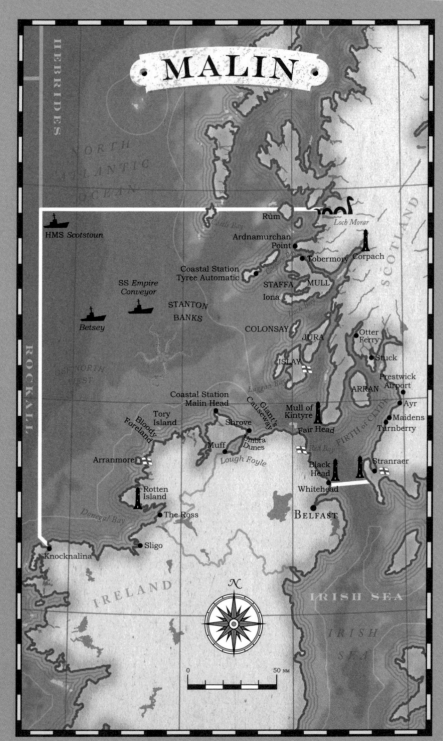

MAP 26

Wind Northeast 5, decreasing 3 to 4
at times later
Sea state Slight or moderate
Weather Showers then fair
Visibility Good, occasionally poor

START

1. Insufficient facilities for the 1988 Winter Olympics

There's foul ground, a big stretch of rocks and often a wicked sou'westerly, so set off with caution.

2. Strange brew?

Conditions on this long leg may turn out very different to those predicted, so make your crossing plan flexible and check for reports from the conveniently nearby Coastal Stations.

3. It's *not* bad language; it's because in the sunset, the rocks are a lovely red

The waters around here are home to many fishing nets and lobster pots, in neither of which you want to get your vessel snarled up.

4. Where You May Find a Heath, or Even an Eden?

(You're on the tip of a lough the ownership of which is, at the moment, quietly – for which we're all mercifully grateful – disputed.)

5. Keep going, but stop just before you reach Ash?

Ever had your field of vision filled with wild orchids, from Early-Purple to Marsh Helleborine, from Bee Orchid to Frog Orchid? Turn to see the dunes on your starboard side; less inspirationally, there's also a castle famous mainly for its kitchen dropping plumb into the sea.

6. In folklore, the setting-off point on a journey to Scotland for creatures so fictitiously *enormous* that they didn't need the Shipping Forecast – or, indeed, ships

Around the island that's coming in to view – where Robert the Bruce met his spider – is a breeding ground for seals and of some of the fiercest rip of tide you'll encounter in this part of these islands.

7. Appropriately, and with apologies, this one is more exposed to the air...

The relevant lighthouse, whose signal reaches 27 nautical miles, gives one white flash every three seconds.

8. ... than this one

The prominent 'Fairy Rock' that will come into view on your port side is the place to get quarrying blue-hone granite for curling stones.

9. Site of a sports venue which was taken over in 2014
by an American who claims Scottish heritage

The harbour you're heading to will hopefully be renovated to
restore it to its nineteenth-century glory – when it was associated
with Scotland's most adept ring-net fishermen – so don't forget to
pay your mooring fee.

10. 'In the highlands, in the country places / Where the
old plain men have rosy faces / And the young fair
____ / Quiet eyes' (Robert Louis Stephenson)

On the shore you're passing is the Electric Brae, named because
the strange contours of this land make uphill look like downhill,
prompting some to posit the existence of invisible forces.

11. It's named after *an* element, but not *that* one
(and not a 'Periodic Table' one)

Fresh southerly winds can cause the seas to break perilously:
you'll find that everything is easier on the east side.

12. The only UK number-one single (so far) to feature a
team of bagpipers from Campbeltown

End

The streaks of foam are dense.
The crests of waves are toppling,
tumbling and rolling. Your visibility
is impeded by sea spray.

HEBRIDES

All those turbines are one clue that there's a *lot* of wind here. Another – more potent – clue is the series of huge gasps and thrusts that will toss you around and about.

There's also an abundance of rocks, as the crew of SS *Politician* discovered in 1941, when that ship ran aground and the nearby islanders 'rescued' its cargo: 22,000 cases of malt whisky, a tale retold in book form as *Whisky Galore* and with an exclamation mark as the film *Whisky Galore!*

The island Eriskay, was also where a privateer took Bonnie Prince Charlie to plot the '45 Jacobite Rising.

Yes, these are edgelands between which you're navigating. Look out to one side, and you'll see exactly the ravishing scenery that the name Hebrides suggests – towering crags alternating with glowing blue lagoons; to the other side, there's often nothing in sight, and that's *without* the knowledge that there's a France or a Germany hiding beyond the horizon. Gaze southwest-ish from St Kilda, for example. The nearest land, 3,700 nautical miles away, is Venezuela.

Turn your head an inch or so, and it's clear water all the way down to the Larsen Ice Shelf in Antarctica.

You're asea, shipmate.

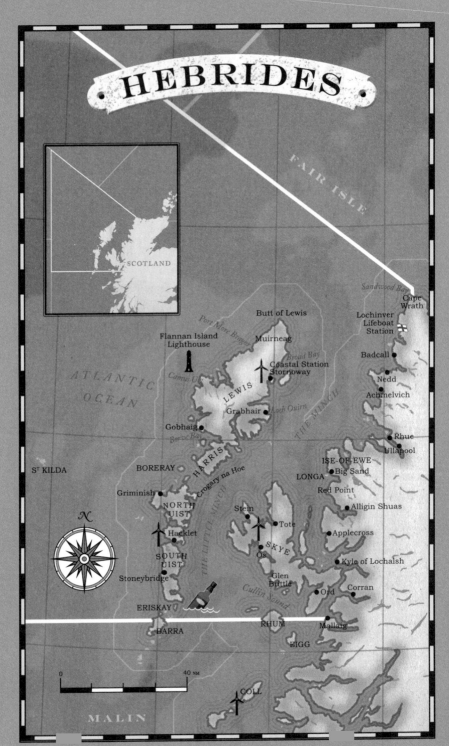

MAP 27

Difficulty
Strong breeze

Wind North or northeast, 8 or 9
Sea state Very rough
Weather Thundery showers
Visibility Poor

START

1. Flandders?

The loch you're crossing is deep enough that it got used as practice for midget submarines in the Second World War: the Commander-in-Chief, Naval Home Command, sent capital ships from his fleet to be used as target practice, which is a good moment to remember to listen on VHF to channel 16 at 0710 and 1910: that's when the coastguard gives the details of what today's subs are doing... today.

2. I disagree with the referee's ruling

Now is your chance to see humpback whales: you're passing a spot where they enjoy leaping through the surface of their world and into ours for a few magical moments; as you approach your destination, you are advised to make a courtesy call to Kilda Radio, again on VHF channel 16.

3. Make Charles yawn

If some of the landscape you're passing looks eerily familiar, that may be because Stanley Kubrick used it in *2001: A Space Odyssey* to stand in for... well, Jupiter.

4. Part of Angela Merkel's photo-ops

Now you're close to where, in *To the Lighthouse,* men are seen 'pitting muscle and brain against the waves and the wind'; whatever you're using, you should be factoring in magnetic variation 3.5 °W.

145

5. Is this your bag?

A long-time home to long-line and drift-net fishers.

6. Pink Smith, perhaps, or Golden Gala

Numerous smallish rocks for you to avoid while gawping at the scenery.

7. Did I hear you right? I just sailed round the whole thing, and it was barely three nautical miles

And now it's getting incredibly shoaly.

8. Half of it's actually stone

NB: Sgeir a' Bhuic is connected to your destination by rocky ledges.

9. Oh, I feel the same way!

Glacier tongues created these sea lochs.

10. Sound of regret

The island you're passing is no longer quarantined, but not everyone is convinced that it's got rid of all that anthrax they tested there in the 1940s, so sail on by and cross The Minch, a strait that's sheltered from big sea swells, but subject to strong winds.

11. First thing a rough barber does

End

· BAILEY ·

There's nothing to see here, even on a clear day.

Today, however, is not a clear day.

You will be navigating the Bailey Shipping Area in a deep, thick fog. So it's time to remind yourself of the COLREGS: the International Regulations for Preventing Collisions at Sea that the International Maritime Organization agreed on in 1972.

Before then, different parts of the world had different conventions to try to avoid vessels ramming into one another; it's not hard to see the problems with *that* kind of ambiguity.

So even the ships with radar will be sounding their horns in line with the COLREGS.

Time to focus.

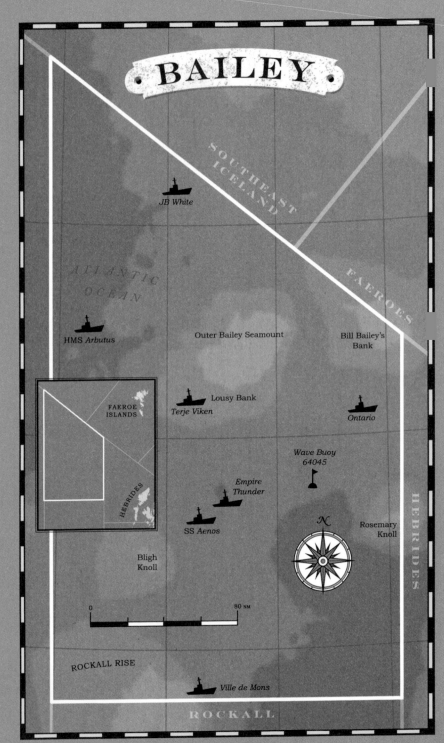

BAILEY

SOUTHEAST ICELAND

JB White

ATLANTIC OCEAN

FAEROES

HMS *Arbutus*

Outer Bailey Seamount

Bill Bailey's Bank

FAEROE ISLANDS

Lousy Bank

Terje Viken

Ontario

HEBRIDES

Wave Buoy 64045

Empire Thunder

N

Rosemary Knoll

SS Aenos

HEBRIDES

Bligh Knoll

0   80 NM

ROCKALL RISE

Ville de Mons

ROCKALL

MAP 28

Difficulty
Fresh gale

Wind Southwest 6 to gale 8
Sea state Mainly slight
Weather Showers for a time
Visibility Very poor

START

1. Christian's enemy

You will know this, of course, but this is a reminder that if another vessel is in distress in this fog, there are signals other than a radiotelephony 'Mayday' and . . . − − −. . . that mean you need to help...

2. Keep near this?

... for example, a smoke signal giving off orange-coloured smoke...

3. Drinker in a song of 1902 AND singer of comedy songs since the 1980s

4. Laertes is reminded that it's for commemoration

... shells firing red stars one at a time at short intervals...

5. On an envelope... ON

... flames from a burning tar barrel, and more.

6. Bloody, froggy, ___

End

FAIR ISLE

It has the *loveliest* name of all the shipping areas. But there is a reason the Shetland island after which it's named is called Fair Isle: that name is some of the Norse you'll be encountering a lot on this voyage, since you're closer to Norway than you are to Edinburgh.

Fair Isle itself, midway between Shetland and Orkney, boasts of being the UK's most remote inhabited island – remote enough that when the Spanish Armada's *El Gran Grifón* was wrecked there in 1588, it remained hidden until, well... 1970.

And *that* Norse name of Fair Isle means 'tranquillity': tranquillity, that is, in comparison to the often wild waters around. Fair Isle has given its name to something as well as a shipping area, of course. And there's a reason those Fair Isle woollens* are *warm.* Consider yourself warned.

Fair Isle could have been deemed part of the Shetlands (just under 21 nautical miles away) or, closer to the mainland, the Orkneys (23 nautical miles). The more distant Shetlands it is, then, so when you imagine this Area, stretch your mind closer to the chilly Faeroes and Iceland than you do to the mainland's John O'Groats.

* Incidentally, if you've heard that grim-but-touching tale where every family has a distinct knitting pattern so that when, inevitably, a sailor's skeleton washed onto the shore, he could be identified... I'm afraid it's a romance.

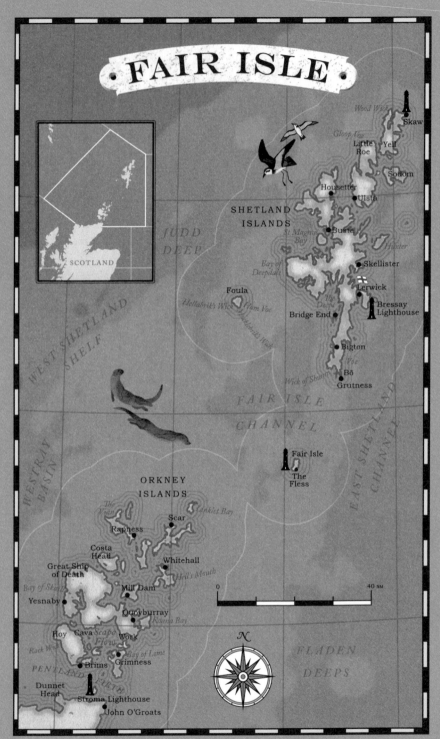

MAP 29

Difficulty
Fresh breeze

Wind Cyclonic, mainly southerly or
southeasterly 4 or 5
Sea state Mainly slight
Weather Showers, rain later
Visibility Good, occasionally poor later

START

1. Divine retribution or not, this place is *very seldom* associated with fire-and-brimstone temperatures

Off to the south of you is Coastal Station Lerwick, whose reports make up part of the extended Shipping Forecast every day.

2. I heard you the first time

On the port side, enjoy the very nice gneiss that blesses your view with pink cliffs.

3. What you can fit on a *tiny* blini

These early legs take you closest to the arctic maritime air mass: as the name suggests, this brings cold air and the likelihood of heavy showers from the North Pole.

4. If they're having trouble recruiting crew, they could always change the vessel's name...

There is a reason for all the lighthouses here, though the local adage 'Samphrey men are always taken by the sea' is not entirely true: in 1832, a storm picked up a boat and carried it from the haaf all the way to Norway; the Norwegians nursed them to health and sent them back to the Shetlands, to the delighted astonishment of their families.

5. CEO of a coffee chain with 8,000 UK outlets?

The causeways on your starboard side were constructed by Italian prisoners-of-war in the 1940s.

6. Word in hit singles for The Verve, Kate Bush, Bryan Ferry... and the Beatles song which was a double-A side with 'Day Tripper'

And if you're considering a spot of light whaling, one of the many (many) reasons to give that a miss is the witch's curse: no whales will be caught here until someone digs up a thimble apparently buried in the sands on the shore many lifetimes ago.

7. Prosecco is to Venetto as ____ is to Catalonia

The lighthouse you'll be using is on an abandoned island where the persistent spray of salty water mummified some of its former inhabitants, making it quite the tourist spot in the 1700s until someone left open the door of the mausoleum and sheep trampled the mummies into dust – all gone.

8. He led out Team GB in 2012

End

FAEROES

The good news is that you will be staying close to shore in this shipping area. The even better news is that the people of the Faeroes are notorious for an intense hospitality, once you get used to the fact that it's too cold for anyone to smile at you for long.

The most pressing news is that this is a stark and rocky bit of ocean, which requires your constant vigilance, especially in poor visibility. Think of it as a section of a ridge which joins Iceland to Scotland, where some cliffs happen to have been tough enough to remain sticking out of the water.

And for your paperwork, remember that while the Faeroes might have been part of the Kingdom of Denmark since 1814, and while Denmark might have joined the European Communities in 1973, the Faeroes are not part of the EU, also, hefty phone roaming charges will apply and they use the *føroysk króna*.

(And on the topic of unfamiliar letters, 'ð' is *really* pronounced 'th' and isn't the 'd' we take it to be in these puzzles.)

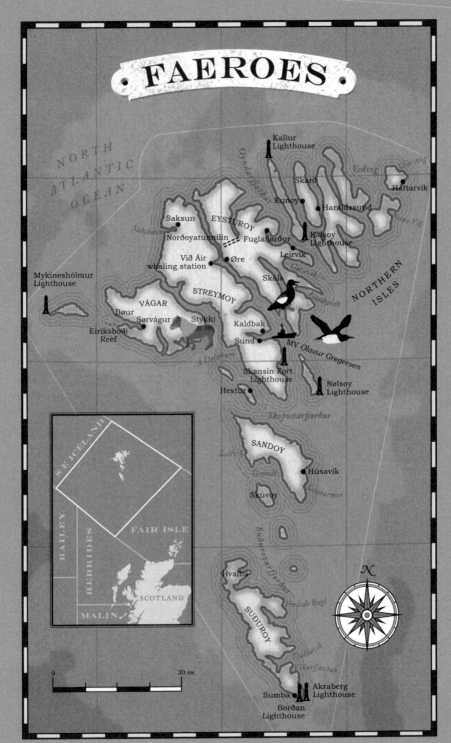

MAP 30

Difficulty
Fresh breeze

Wind Variable 3 to 4 at first in north,
otherwise northeasterly 5 to 6
Sea state Moderate or rough
Weather Wintry showers
Visibility Moderate or poor,
occasionally good

START

1. It's actually pronounced like the name of a war that ended with British control of the Transvaal, 1910 (or, if you insist, a porcine male)

Head to the north: you'll be rounding Vágur along its northern coast. There's a hidden reef here known as Eiriksboði, named in memory of a legendary Eirikur who a bishop forgave for quite a shocking sin (killing his brother), so long as the bishop got a fat ox once per annum. God, apparently not keen on this shady arrangement, essentially created the reef solely in order to drown Eirikur – so watch out.

2. It absolutely is *not* tacky!

You can get eddies around this island, especially if the northwestern current has been running past for an hour or more.

3. Two ingredients of soy?

The word 'foul' is often used to describe some of the channels you'll be passing, and with reason.

4. Sounds like a venue for the premieres of *Otello,
Norma, Turandot* and *Madama Butterfly*

Finally, back down the channel you just navigated, and north,
north; be aware of submarine cables as you approach your stark
and final destination.

5. ... for life?

End

SOUTHEAST ICELAND

Southeast Iceland is special among the Shipping Forecast areas: it has its *own* category alongside visibility, sea state and the ones you've got used to...

... 'icing'.

This is when mighty winds and cold waters combine to produce a black and, yes, icy crust on your rigging and superstructure, enough sometimes to capsize your vessel. Sea smoke is *not* your friend.

You'll notice that *your* forecasts for Southeast Iceland do not mention *icing*, which is because *I* wouldn't want you to travel in those conditions. For this voyage, you're going to be feeling the mitigating effects of the Gulf Stream: sometimes, the temperature might even rise above zero.

Finally, as a British boat in Icelandic waters, please be overly courteous to any local vessels you pass. Memories are strong here, as we'll see, of Icelandic boats encountering British ones and getting... rammed.

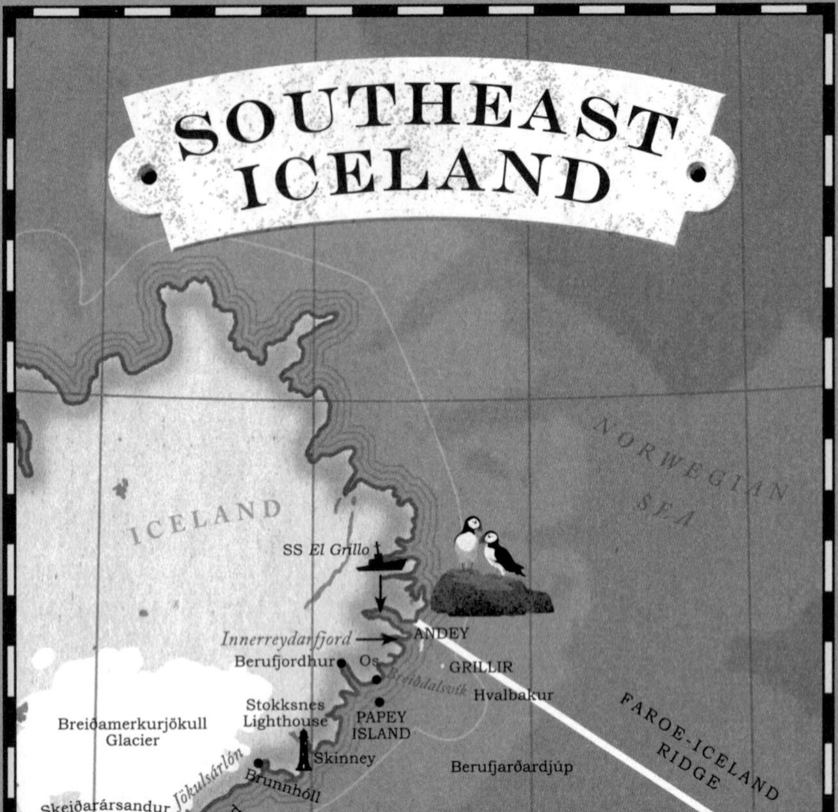

SOUTHEAST ICELAND

NORWEGIAN SEA

ICELAND

SS *El Grillo*

ANDEY

Innerreydarfjord →

Berufjordhur • Os

GRILLIR

Breiðdalsvík

Hvalbakur

Stokksnes
Lighthouse

Breiðamerkurjökull
Glacier

PAPEY
ISLAND

FAROE-ICELAND
RIDGE

Jökulsárlón

Skinney

Brunnhóll

Berufjarðardjúp

Skeiðarársandur

Hof

Diamond
Beach

Markbót

Kirkjubæjarklaustur

Lónsdjúp

HMS *Rawalpindi*

Hornafjarðardjúp

Skeiðarárdjúp   Breiðamerkurdjúp

𝒩

ICELAND
BASIN

NORTH

ATLANTIC

OCEAN

BAILEY

FAEROES

0   100 NM

MAP 31

Difficulty
Moderate gale

Wind Southwesterly backing
southerly later, 6 to 7
Sea state Rough, occasionally moderate
Weather Wintry showers
Visibility Good occasionally moderate

START

1. Yes, it really *is* a long name, but if you look really closely at it, it's because its terrain makes it look like a church... specifically a cloister

If that glacier you're passing might look familiar, it's because you saw it in the pre-title sequence of *A View to a Kill* and in the billionaire's ice-palace scene of *Die Another Day.*

2. Sounds like something said to a barista

The large-ish fishing town you're about to pass, which styles itself the Lobster Capital, is also the starting-off point for tourists zipping about on amphibians and zodiacs.

3. Brother to Bårrey, Røbíen and Måúrīece?

There are strong tidal currents here, sometimes reaching six knots on the ebb; watch out for breakers.

4. Like Giórge Föreman, famously?

You're heading into waters which were contested in the Cod Wars of the 1950s, '60s and '70s when, with fishing rights under dispute, Royal Navy vessels took to ramming Icelandic fishing boats, sometimes resulting in the letting off of live ammunition.

5. It was named for a Punjab city

Don't disturb the great auks, happily breeding and not especially used to observing visitors.

6. Its name means 'Whale's Back' and it is Iceland's most easterly point

Over on your port side is Papey Island, named for the Papar, the incredibly hardy Irish monks who sailed here before the Vikings did.

7. They're worth six points each in Icelandic Scrabble

End

SOLUTIONS

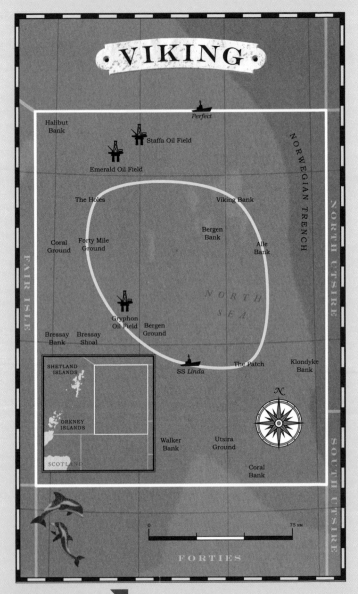

Viking Voyage: O 361 nautical miles

As you can see, it's not a *perfect* O. There's only one other O voyage, in fact; most of the journeys involve straighter – if wonky – lines

VIKING VOYAGE

The Holes, an area of the North Sea's bed that looks *exactly* like you'd expect from the name; now, as you've seen, a '____' in a clue could mean a gap of one word, or of two, or more; the mayor, by the way, is trying to battle the rats in Browning's *The Pied Piper of Hamelin.*

Viking Bank, a seamount well known among mariners which was chosen as the name for a new Shipping Area when Forties was split in two; in those few Shipping Areas which – like Viking – lack land altogether, we'll be encountering banks, shoals, oil rigs and other things that in real life you might prefer to quite literally steer clear of (sometimes the clues refer explicitly to words like 'Bank' and 'Ground' – but *most often* they don't).

Alle Bank: 'alle' is German for 'all', hence '*entirely* in German': some of the foreign names are, like this, clued by what they mean, and much more often *what they look like they might mean.*

The Patch: Sir Arthur preferred this novel, *The White Company*, to his Holmes tales: here's a flavour: 'We went forth in little ships and came back in great galleys — for of fifty tall ships of Spain, over two score flew the Cross of St. George ere the sun had set.'

SS *Linda* was attacked in 1940 by the U-boat *U-9*; all but one of the crew were rescued by the Swedish vessel *Birgitta*; the clue is one of the lateral-thinking ones, here the first names of the spouses of John, Paul, George and Ringo at the end of the Beatles era.

Gryphon oil field: the mythological creature is sometimes spelled 'griffon' or 'griffin', but this is the best version.

Forty Mile Ground, alluding, as we will often do, to a song, in this case 'I'm Gonna Be (500 Miles)'.

The Holes again!

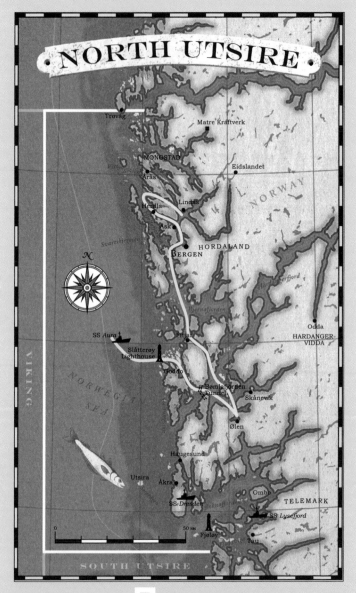

North Utsire Voyage: S ■ **221 nautical miles**

You started at a refinery and ended at a shipwreck, but your travels between should, I hope, have imparted to you some of the quiet majesty of the fjords which inspired local lad Edvard Grieg.

Lindås, of which those women are three exåmples, give or take a ring diacritic or three; the Lindås refineries produce diesel, jet fuel and petrol coke, all from the North Sea.

Herdla: Akabusi medalled as a 'hurdler' in the 1992 Barcelona Olympics.

Ask (Jeeves being a former search engine), whence the big-city folk of Bergen get their strawberries.

Ølen, long known for its handy quays and decent anchorages.

Goddo (look away if you haven't seen the play, but the title character in *Waiting for Godot* does not appear); Bømlo, where you are, was one end of the Shetland Bus, the Second World War special-ops link between Shetland and Norway, operating in disguise as fishing boats.

SS *Aura*, sunk by a U-boat in August 1915; all crew survived.

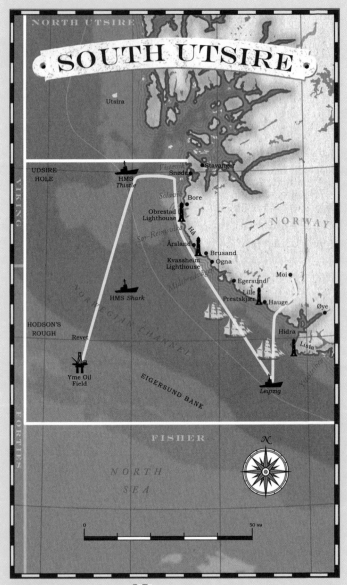

South Utsire Voyage: N ♟️ **198 nautical miles**

A mere 198 nautical miles! An absolute snap? Not with the
navigation demanded of you, and now you can sip a ***brennevin*** and
reflect on your journey which took you from a charming and tiny
hydroelectric station to the stark – possibly grim – remains of a
cracked oil platform.

Moi, which uses the power of the water to keep itself going with a dinky hydroelectric station.

Leipzig, a German cruiser which was battered so often by the Allies that after the Second World War, she was unromantically used as a barracks ship during minesweeping before being unceremoniously scuttled at this very spot.

Brusand (Bruce and Tess, the original *Strictly* hosts): these obstacles were erected by Norwegian prisoners-of-war, who slyly and intentionally used a form of concrete with too much sand, rendering many of them pleasingly and completely useless.

Hå ('ha!'), responsible for both the wonderful Kvassheim and Obrestad lighthouses.

Bore, which has *some* rips and undertow if you're tempted to ride the froth.

Snøde ('snowed'): in fact, the warming gulf stream makes this edge of Norway a little rainier and a little less *snowy* than others – *but*, when that sea snow comes, you *know* about it.

HMS *Thistle* (those countries' national emblems), a sturdy T-class submarine of 1,500 tons.

Yme ('Why me?'): the depth of the Norwegian Trench means there aren't so many pipelines around *these* parts; Yme was abandoned in 2001 after 14 years, but more recently became Norway's first oil field to attract people willing to give it a second crack.

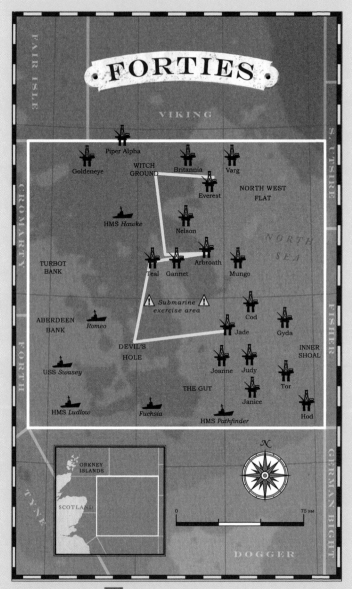

Forties Voyage: E ▮▮ **299 nautical miles**

A potentially horrendous business, avoiding tankers you can't see until you're close to them: but with a reasonable sea state and assured navigation, you completed your voyage with aplomb.

Jade: women's names roughly corresponding to the colours of the rainbow: Enron's untimely investment in the J-Block of oil fields is a small part of its massive collapse.

Devil's Hole, a group of trenches 80 fathoms deeper than anything else around, given its name by fishermen sick and tired of losing their trawl nets on its steep sides: a Notice to Mariners concerning this phenomenon was issued by the Admiralty in 1930 after a re-charting of the area by HM Survey Ship *FitzRoy* – named in honour of the creator of the Shipping Forecast.

Teal: the waterfowl whose colouring, in the twentieth century, gave a name to another kind of green to join jade above.

Arbroath oil field: 110 or so nautical miles to the west, they claim, a shop caught fire, meaning that the barrels of salted haddock got so hot that the fish was cooked and the Arbroath Smokie was accidentally invented.

Gannet oil field: in 2013, the journal *Science*, concerned that we know more about what seabirds do over land than when they're actually at sea, had a proper gander at some gannets: despite their reputation for greed, the colonies have clearly defined and mutually respected fishing grounds.

Witch Ground, a large basin pockmarked all over with greenhouse gases.

Everest oil field; Mauna Kea is so hulking that it depresses the ocean floor in Hawaii by about 3,000 fathoms.

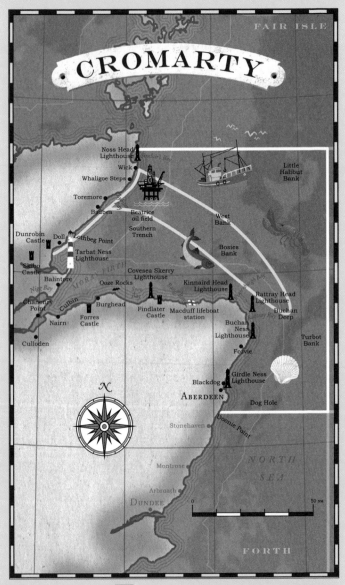

Cromarty Voyage: P ☐ **210 nautical miles**

And if you wish, you could now change vessels and travel down
Thomas Telford's Caledonian Canal to the Malin shipping area,
on the other side of the mainland: if so, *bon voyage*!

Dunrobin Castle, which has been continually inhabited for eight centuries, has its own train station and was a naval hospital during the first world war.

Doll, a spread-out triangular crofting township just down the coast from a Second World War radio station that intercepted messages from Germany to Norway for the benefit of Bletchley Park; Cliff took 'Living Doll' to the top with the Drifters in 1959 and with the Young Ones in 1986 and had *previously* released a different song called 'Livin' Lovin' Doll' in a futile attempt to stop 'Living Doll' (which he didn't much care for) being released.

Wick, which had 1,100 boats exporting fish as far as the West Indies during its Victorian heyday, following the relocation from the west coast – to these waters – of shoals of herring; some fisherwomen arrived in Wick having carried their fish baskets up that 'manmade stairway' mentioned, the 365-stair Whaligoe Steps, then having walked the remaining eight miles.

West Bank, you're now in international waters, just southwest of Little Halibut Bank; NB if you find yourself approaching a *colder* Little Halibut Bank, you have gone *seriously* astray and are off the coast of Greenland on the path followed by Amundsen when traveling the Northwest Passage: take *urgent* action.

Buchan Deep, with reference to John Buchan, who wrote *Naval Episodes of the Great War* as well as such thrillers as *The Thirty-Nine Steps*.

Beatrice oil field: to be precise, Beatrice was the second of renowned oilman T. Boone Pickens' five spouses at the time of writing; with the oil all gone, what you are looking at from your boat is the area's reimagining as a deep-water wind farm which hopes to power half a million homes.

Badbea ('bad bee'), whose last inhabitant left in 1911; now a grim tourist attraction commemorating those who were forced there by the Highland Clearances.

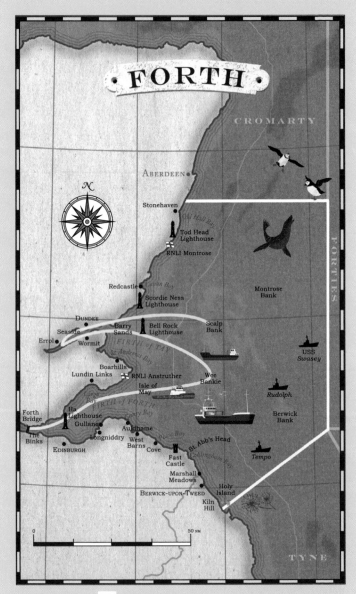

Forth Voyage: S ■ **352 nautical miles**
Mostly spent in the busy River Tay and busier still Firth of Forth,
you hopefully had a moment or two at the end where you didn't
have to think about having many other vessels in all directions.

FORTH VOYAGE

Forth Bridge, which has over 6½ million rivets; Network Rail announced in 2011 that the bridge would not need another lick of paint until 2036 (and just to spoil the old metaphor one more time, the maintenance crews used to attend to the most weather-beaten areas first, rather than mindlessly proceeding from one side to the other).

Largo Bay, where a naval commander ordered the building of a canal starting at his country pile so that he could arrive by boat at church on Sundays; also home to the real-life Robinson Crusoe, the privateer Alexander Selkirk; music is the famous Largo from Dvořák's *New World Symphony*.

Isle of May: three weeks of the month of May see Taurus births, followed by a fair few Geminis.

Wee Bankie, home to sand eels which provide supper for the area's top predators.

Wormit, where various Norwegian boats spent the Second World War (oh, and let's not forget the King of Norway, who led the resistance against Quisling from dear Wormit).

Seaside: 'fairly' because you might argue it could be called Tayside.

Errol, as in Flynn, who did some acting when he wasn't having fun on his various mammoth yachts (portraying Fletcher Christian, Don Juan and Robin Hood among others).

Scalp: indeed, *don't* hang around here for long.

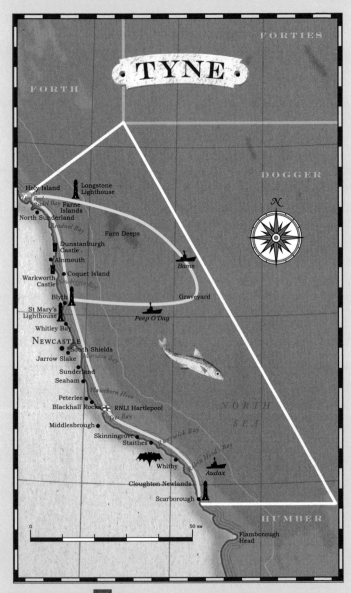

TYNE

FORTIES

FORTH

DOGGER

Holy Island
Longstone Lighthouse
The Peel
Ridal Bay
Farne Islands
North Sunderland
Beadnel Bay
Farn Deeps
Dunstanburgh Castle
Alnmouth
Bams
Warkworth Castle
Coquet Island
Blyth
Graveyard
St Mary's Lighthouse
Whitley Bay
Peep O'Day
NEWCASTLE
South Shields
Jarrow Slake
Sunderland
Seaham
Peterlee
Blackhall Rocks
RNLI Hartlepool
Middlesbrough
Skinningrove
Staithes
Whitby
Audax
Cloughton Newlands
Scarborough

NORTH SEA

HUMBER

Flamborough Head

0   50 NM

Tyne Voyage: P ▢ 201 nautical miles

From Dracula's haunting ground, right up to the home of some
1,300-year-old gospels and a proper spot of North Sea, before safe
haven at the mouth of a river with a reassuring name.

Scarborough: the melody of the ballad 'Scarborough Fair' is hundreds of years old, though the herbs only became part of it in the nineteenth century.

Robin Hood's Bay: unconnected with any Merry Men, the name probably pays tribute to local friendly forest elves.

Whitby, which Bram Stoker used as a base to write a story he had planned about a 'Count Wampyr'; Whitby's beach, locals say, inspired Lewis Carroll's 'The Walrus and the Carpenter' and *Moby-Dick* pays tribute to such Whitby mariners as Captain Scoresby (on the subject of the Greenland whale, 'he is the best existing authority'), who came up with the idea of sticking someone in a barrel tied to a mast... latterly known as a 'crow's nest'.

Middlesbrough: local lore says that a misspelling of 'Middlesborough' by the town clerk when applying for 'municipal borough' status led to the 'o'-depleted version becoming the official name.

Jarrow: at the end of the Jarrow March of 1936, the Crusaders were kindly gifted rail tickets back to the Tyne.

Coquet Island, managed by the RSPB and peopled by its wardens in summer; since the lighthouse is automated, the island can remain uninhabited in winter; 'coquet' was used before the 'coquette' version we're familiar with today.

North Sunderland, 60 miles from Sunderland; the overlap is a bizarre coincidence, since the *city*'s name means 'estate that's cast asunder', whereas *this little fishing village*'s name means, well, there's no easy way to say this: 'north south land'.

Lindisfarne, aka Holy Island: the album and the Gazza single mentioned are both 'Fog on the Tyne'.

Graveyard, a bank near to shipping area Dogger which, happily, is not littered with wrecks; you happen to be near the Norwegian sailing vessel *Bams*, downed in 1916 by a U-boat; happily, all the crew survived.

Blyth, named because its river was thought to be, well, gentle; the port has survived the decline of coal and shipbuilding because it's where pulp arrives from Scandinavia for the hanging-in-there industry of... um, newspapers.

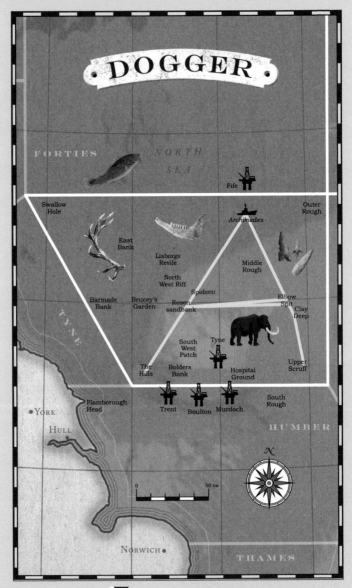

Dogger Voyage: A 354 nautical miles
And to think you could have once done the whole thing on foot
(407 land miles)...

DOGGER VOYAGE

Upper Scruff (as in scruff of the neck): a bank you will wish to factor in to your navigation.

Clay Deep: a hole made of 'hot shale'; reference to Cassius Clay.

Rosen sandbank: paraphrase of Michael Rosen's folk-song adaptation *We're Going on a Bear Hunt*.

Elbow Spit: the macaroni and this spur both take the shape of a bent arm.

SS *Archimedes*, one of the first steamships, named after the 'Eureka!' genius, was constructed in South Shields; in 1864, her engine wasn't up to the storm she encountered and she ran aground here. All were saved and, for extra safety, dynamite was used to strew *Archimedes* in smaller pieces all around the bed.

The Hills, undeniably alive in the opening words of *The Sound of Music*.

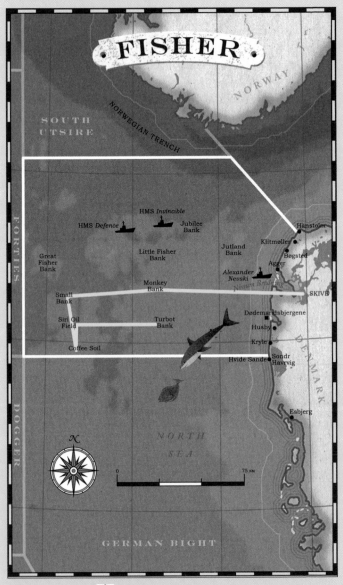

Fisher Voyage: F ◆ **272 nautical miles**

And let's not pretend we don't know why Northumberland ended up using a Nordic word in that first clue: no disrespect, but you've just successfully navigated what the Vikings regarded as merely a hop, skip and a jump to our isles.

Skive: listen, if you're tempted to delay setting sail because you've heard that the local limestone caves are full of ageing and delicious *Cavecheese* for export to Germany: well, yes they are, but those same caves are also home to tens of thousands of upside-down bats; incidentally, they say that an English word 'skive' comes from the Norse – but it's *not* the one in the clue, meaning 'malinger'; instead it's a technical description involving the splitting of leather which made it from Scandinavia to Northumberland, but not much further.

Monkey Bank ('monkey' = slang for £500); want to feel like you're already, on this voyage, freakily far from what's familiar? Monkey Bank is one of the best locations if you're interested in an excellent clam with the excellent name ocean quahog, which truly takes its time. Its lifespan? At *least* half a millennium. In your face, tortoises.

Small Bank (reference: the irrepressible Small Clanger): yes, cute name but, as a mariner, you're smart enough to recognise that if the nautical chart reads 'Some-Have-Survived Shoal', 'Barely Fatal Reef', or even 'Teeny-Weeny Ridge', it's still worth navigating around.

Coffee Soil: *do* rake out those grounds if you're a horticulturist when you're a landlubber.

Siri oil field, which shares a name with Apple's virtual-assistant contemporary of Alexa and the other creepy IT pals on offer.

Turbot Bank: even since that Turbot War mentioned, overfishing has led to Canadian seizures of EU vessels; the overfishing issue may be long decided here in Fisher but continued closer to Newfoundland.

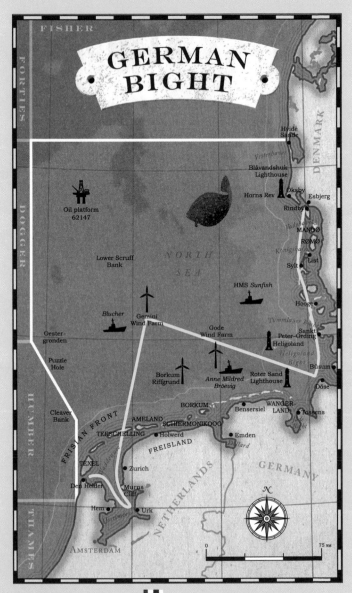

German Bight Voyage: N 🏁 **330 nautical miles**

... and without running aground once. The old navigators of these parts look on you with admiration.

GERMAN BIGHT VOYAGE

Den Helder, whose naval dockyard was built at Napoleon's behest; '(Dirty) Den held 'er'.

Hem, on the sheltered western side of the lake.

Urk ('irk'), once an island in the Almere lake, and still an island up until 1939, at which point a dyke rendered it part of the mainland.

Zurich (approx. pop.: 190).

Gemini, our planet's third-largest offshore wind farm; Castor and Pollux are the 'twins' of Gemini.

Döse, where the Elbe finishes its 691-mile-journey from whatever the Czech Republic is called nowadays.

Büsum, home to the *Kutterregatta* and another one-time island.

Hooge, which grandly presents itself as the Queen of the Halligen.

Sylt (which is a kind of herring) was once reachable on foot, was for a spell protected from erosion by a series of 'tetrapods' (basically enormous concrete bollards) and is now kept intact by getting the sand back out of the sea and replacing it on the beaches (annual cost, a mere €10 million).

Rindby, on Fanø, an island with a long maritime history where those westerlies mean that that while there are a *lot* of pine trees, they're none of them very tall.

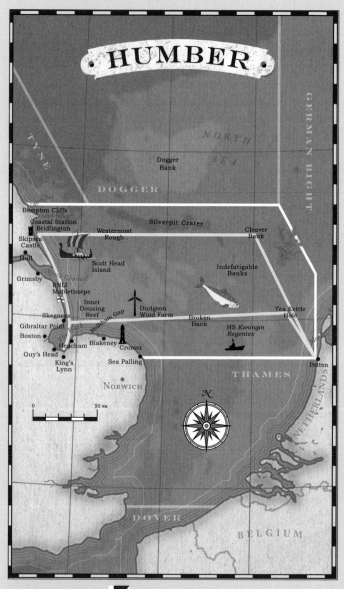

Humber Voyage: A **442 nautical miles**

And you're right, it wasn't *all* flat: you have the memories of such fine views as Holkham Gap and Bempton Cliffs as well as *occasional* spells of monotony.

King's Lynn, once known merely as Bishop's Lynn, though it was still pretty swank in those days, thanks to a ton of Hanseatic League booty.

Skegness, home of the first Butlin's; Bert thinks of it as 'Skeggy'; one of its grander monikers is 'the Blackpool of the East Coast' and one of its *even less* grand ones is 'Costa del Skeg'.

Skipsea Castle, built to keep out the Danes, although it has to be said that there's a certain irony in its name – *Skip sær* – being originally a way of saying 'This Is Where We Scandinavians Moor Our Ships'.

Cleaver Bank, deep enough that its cobbly bottom resists the movement of the waves, meaning that it provides a home for dead man's finger (an astonishing coral) and a happy spawning ground (if you're a herring).

Petten (pet #10), where a 250kg basking shark got fatally lost in 2004 and has been on ice ever since, awaiting a more lasting display solution; much of the Dutch coast remains largely invisible from seaward.

Tea Kettle Hole, name-checked in the ancient Lowestoft shanty in praise of fishing alone in a single boat rather than 'fleeting': 'We'll go down to the Knoll or the Tea Kettle Hole / And anywhere else in the sea / We'll mind the trawl net / While the owner's abed / But none of your fleeting for me'.

Dudgeon, which is about as far offshore as UK wind farms get.

Gibraltar Point, famous for its wildfowl as well as for being one end of 'Gibraltar Point to North Foreland' in the Inshore Waters section of the Shipping Forecast.

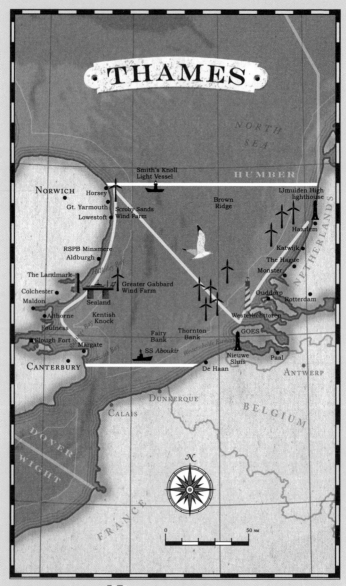

Thames Voyage: N **312 nautical miles**

You did not run aground on the Kentish Knoll. You did not break the various Belgian rules regarding red diesel and wind farms. And you did not get tempted to go and live on the Principality of Sealand. Success!

THAMES VOYAGE

Sandwich Bay: the snack is named after the earl whose earldom was named after the place which is named after what you find on the beach and don't want to let into the snack.

Margate, as featured in the typically inspiring words from *The Waste Land*: 'On Margate sands / I can connect / Nothing with nothing'.

Foulness, protected by the Ministry of Defence (because of the weapons research, not because of the avocets), which actually just means 'promontory which birds enjoy hanging out at'.

Maldon, home of chi-chi salt and featured in the Old English poem 'The Battle of Maldon', where Byrhtnoth and his friend Ælfric fail to stave off the Northmen.

The Landmark, also known as Naze Tower, which used to have a beacon to guide vessels through the shoaly area of the Goldmer Gap... yes, it was basically a lighthouse (and Naze means 'nose', from the beaky shape of the nearby coast).

Horsey: even in smuggling's heyday, there was little in East Anglia. The contraband that did make its way onshore here was taken up the Norfolk Broads, where the wherrymen used the sails of local mills as a signal that customs men were around: a signal that could pass miles inland *way* faster than any customs man could travel.

Goes, site of a siege relieved in 1572 when the Spanish literally waded across the River Scheldt to fight off the Dutch and keep it part of the Spanish Netherlands.

Monster, as in 'monastery': Monster was a pilgrimage town.

The Hague or, in the local language, The Hedge; maybe some day it will simply be Hedge, just as our own The Bath lost its definite article.

Haarlem: before the Dutch arrived in Harlem, that part of America area was occupied by the Manhattan tribe, but the English burned the whole place to the ground.

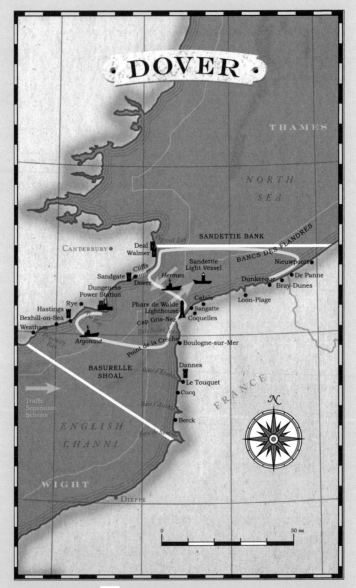

Dover Voyage: S ■ 153 nautical miles

You've visited three different countries, proved the superiority of maritime travel to any other, seen some of the oldest lighthouses for miles around... and deeply alarmed the captains of a lot of commercial vessels.

Dunkerque; that cinematic depiction of Operation Dynamo, *Dunkirk*, was also filmed in Swanage (Portland shipping area), Weymouth (same) and Urk (German Bight).

Nieuwpoort, which of course translates as 'new port', and, with 2,000 berths, announces itself as Europe's largest yachting marina.

Deal, where the extraordinary castle has six rounded bastions flanking another six semi-circular bastions; Noel Edmonds presented *Deal or No Deal*.

South Foreland, whose lighthouse, once powered by sperm oil, warns mariners of that perilous chalk platform, the Goodwin Sands.

White Cliffs of Dover (Dover, by the way, meaning 'the Waters')…

… to **Sangatte** is the undersea part, and your journey still traces the correct shape even if you eagerly started at Folkestone or ended at Calais or Coquelles.

Pointe de la Crèche, since Napoleonic times the site of various forts: you can still see the foundations of the offshore one.

Argonaut, as in Jason and…; the one *you're* over was a cruise ship which was accidentally rammed during breakfast by the Newcastle steamer *Kingswell*; the lifeboats were filled in the shortest time possible and *everyone* made it to shore.

Hastings, which boasts the Hastings Country Park Local Nature Reserve and was the site of a motte-and-bailey castle, as seen in *that* tapestry.

Rye, which sounds like 'wry' and has a noble history as a replacement member of the Cinque Ports when New Romney's harbour silted up.

Dungeness B power station; Dungeness A was decommissioned in 2006.

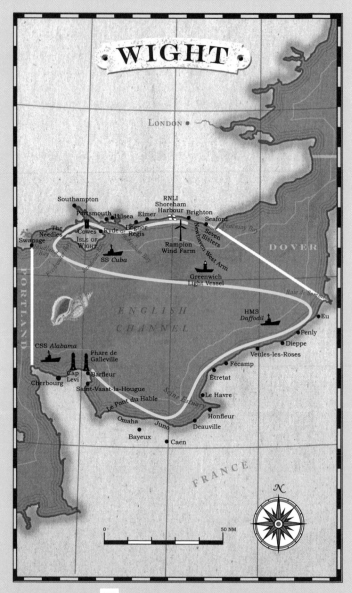

Wight Voyage: S ■ **258 nautical miles**

Perhaps you were hoping to pop inland to Bayeux to mark one of the more celebrated Channel crossings? Why don't you do that right now?

WIGHT VOYAGE

Brighton: see also *Pride and Prejudice, Quadrophenia,* etc.

Elmer, whose wooden groynes failed to keep sea from splitting beach; the other is a patchwork elephant.

Bognor Regis: the king's dodgy doctor chose Bognor for a rest cure because his mate Sir Arthur du Cros had a stately home here.

Hilsea (anagrams), on northern tip of Portsea Island.

Ryde: Paul said 'Ticket to Ride' was inspired by a British Rail ticket with destination Ryde; Wight has a splendid mediaeval lighthouse built by a Lord of Chale as apology for buying wine from wreckers.

Cowes, strongly identified with regattas since early-1800s Prince Regent took to mucking about here.

The Needles: there was once a fourth Needle, Lot's Wife, which was much more needle-y.

Studland Bay: before the 1801 foundation of Bournemouth, this chine-banked coast was unpopulated, barren and consequently deeply popular among smugglers.

Eu; coordinates refer to EU Treaty of Maastricht.

Le Havre ('The Harbour') which of course has long kept connections to similarly on-the-nose-named Portsmouth.

Juno: D-Day landings at Juno beach took place in June.

Phare de Galleville, the world's third-largest traditional lighthouse, with an impressive 1,600-watt xenon lamp.

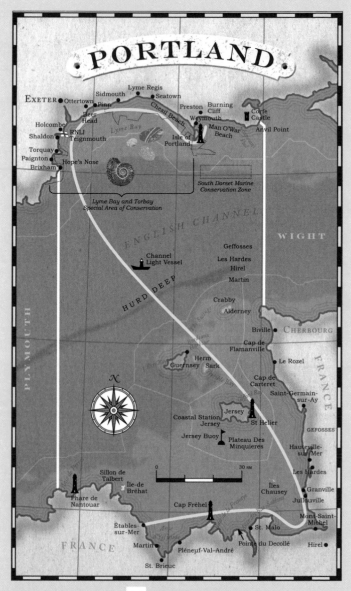

Portland Voyage #1: S ▪ 277 nautical miles
If you made it safely ploughing through all those shipping lanes, and somehow managed to get safely in and out of the Baie de Mont-Saint-Michel, I tip my captain's hat to you.

PORTLAND VOYAGE 1

Preston, of which our British islands have at least a dozen, as priests historically enjoyed setting up farms, and 'Preston' means 'priest's farm'. *This* Preston is a suburb of Weymouth, which has a tourist sign celebrating the 1348 arrival in the port, from France – having travelled through the Portland shipping area – of... the Black Death.

Chesil Beach: 'stole' because after McEwan mentioned these keepsakes on *Start the Week*, Weymouth and Portland council threatened him with a £2,000 fine: the novelist then arranged for the return of the purloined pebbles; the Booker-nominated novella, *On Chesil Beach*, is set in a time when many newlyweds were perfectly happy with a Dorset resort rather than insisting on three weeks in the Maldives.

Lyme Regis: celebrated, defended and depicted by *French Lieutenant* author John Fowles, the scare quotes are in the clue because it's really not the most imposing of rivers or mouths and is sometimes spelled 'Lym'.

Beer Head: sadly, Devon's village of Beer is not the birthplace of beer, which is probably Iran.

Torquay, whose real-life Gleneagles Hotel famously inspired *Fawlty Towers*.

Bordeaux Harbour on Guernsey: the 'real' Bordeaux is of course in the Biscay shipping area.

Sark: the rhyme should have stopped you sailing to nearby and similarly car-free Herm, though you'll have traced the correct letter in your overall journey if you did so; Sark is also the world's first island to completely eliminate light pollution.

Granville fancies itself 'the Monaco of the North' because it's on a rocky promontory, but the weather is still... Normandy weather.

Mont-Saint-Michel, where our disclaimer that this puzzle book is not to be used for real-life navigation applies triple; the best way of arriving there really is at low tide, on foot.

Étables-sur-Mer, where you can now enjoy la Plage des Godelins, which has had splendid bathing huts since Victorian times.

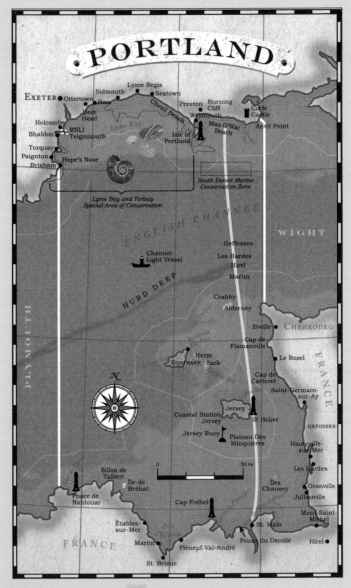

Portland Voyage #2: I ● **119 nautical miles**

Literally very straightforward, from the 51st parallel north down to the 49th, more or less, and more or less on the same longitude.

PORTLAND VOYAGE 2

Man O' War Beach: the Portuguese Man O' War jellyfish is named after a fighting ship; hopefully you will encounter neither.

Alderney (specifically its easternmost point), where you spend, to be specific again, Alderney pounds.

Jersey, which gives its name to both a woolly jumper and a dinky cow.

St Malo, an anagram of 'almost'; the Falklands are named after St Malo, at least in Argentina; gunfire from British boats nearly demolished the walled city in 1944; happily, you are travelling in peacetime.

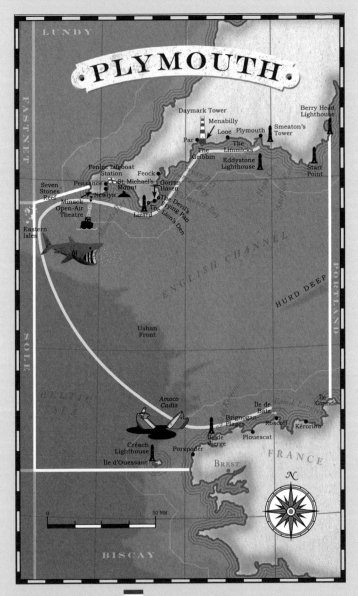

Plymouth Voyage: C ▤ **232 nautical miles**

Happily for you, the line which divides Plymouth from Lundy arrives pretty much at Land's End, so you have been spared the intricate manoeuvring around that headland; not that this journey was exactly simple, so kudos to you.

PLYMOUTH VOYAGE

Plymouth Hoe where most likely Sir Francis wasn't playing at all; besides, the smart move was to wait for wind and tide to change before countering an Armada.

Looe: both these loos are in West Looe; others can be found in East Looe.

Par: Par Harbour ('Harbour Harbour') brought in china clay and the beach turned white from the factories' dust.

The Devil's Frying Pan: blowhole named for its mad 'sizzle' as it spits water like an English geyser.

Lizard; Du Maurier's home was Menabilly and the blowhole is the Lion's Den.

Mounts Bay which, as winter arrives, is consumed by onshore gales.

St Michael's Mount: in 2000, M&S announced 'we are not losing St Michael' shortly before losing it.

Penzance: the 'very model of a modern Major-General' bargains with the *Pirates of Penzance* in the Gilbert & Sullivan comic opera; tidal observatory is at Newlyn.

Minack Theatre, location for that play in 1932 and summer open-air venue since.

Eastern Isles: edge of Scillies that creeps out of Sole; uninhabited, so don't expect to get comfy.

Île de Vierge as opposed to Virgin Islands; wreck is *Amoco Cadiz* supertanker which split in two in 1978 letting loose 220,000 tons of oil.

Île de Batz which survived on the seaweed trade until some of its sailors returned very rich: to this day, you're more likely to see the odd tractor than a car.

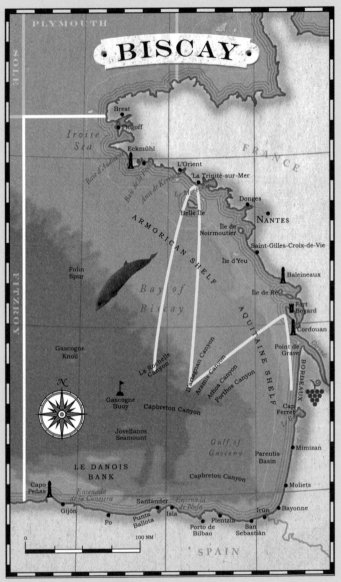

Biscay Voyage #1: M 431 nautical miles
Hoping you didn't get déjà vu during that last leg.

Bordeaux: in the seventeenth century, if you were a European and you were enjoying some coffee, cocoa, sugar or cotton, chances are it got to you via Bordeaux.

Fort Boyard: before being used by the entertainment complex, this was a military base and military prison; Louis XIV's chief military engineer was not hopeful about the construction, telling the king: 'Grabbing the moon with your teeth would be easier than building a thing like *that* in a place like *this*.'

D'Artagnan Canyon: the name was granted because the real Musketeers were from the land 80 or so nautical miles to the east.

La Trinité-sur-Mer: Maud Fontenoy, the first woman to row the Atlantic, followed more or less the Kon-Tiki route and her boat, the *Océor*, was fitted at this port's Marine Technology Yard.

La Rochelle Canyon: together with the canyons above, we're towards the end of a continental shelf which in real life, you would *not* be making a must-see destination.

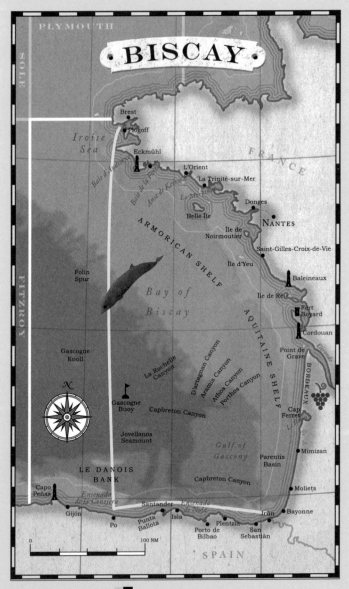

Biscay Voyage #2: L ⬛ 484 nautical miles

Because if you're going to undertake two voyages in Biscay, why **not** have one of them traverse the entire Bay of Biscay?

Brest, home to a quadrennial tall ships meeting and a key port ever since 1631, when Cardinal Richelieu ordered the construction of some wooden wharves.

Po: variously, a river that flows into the Adriatic, a Teletubby and a town that boasts of having the shortest name in Spain.

Santander, which is *quite* the des res for an ancient settler, on the sheltered side of the bay, with a hillside to spot any approaching baddies: a harbour gifted by nature.

Isla: you'll know you're at the right village if you see an enormous residential building which looks like a cross between an observatory and an armadillo.

Porto de Bilbao: Sure enough, the first ports were in the old town, but now the action takes place up here, where they're constantly blowing up the surrounding hills to get materials to build more and more commercial docks.

Irun ('I run', with reference to Paula Radcliffe), meaning that your journey finishes just a few yards short of a return to La Belle France.

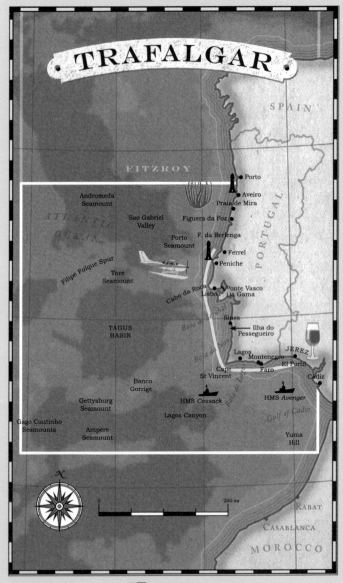

Trafalgar Voyage #1: L ◼ **287 nautical miles**
Some tricky navigation needed at times, but never straying far
from the coast, you've bravely made it from Spain halfway along
the Portuguese littoral without event

Jerez, which gave its name to the lovely libation we call sherry. For a long time, sherry drunk in Britain avoided these exotic names and the stubbornly sweet tipples were known as (a) 'brown' or (b) 'cream'.

Faro, which takes its name from the same kind of monarch as one of the other shipping areas.

Montenegro: the country has been independent since 2006 and, like *this* Montenegro, takes its name from a black mountain.

Lagos, home to Henry the Navigator, who assembled the finest nautical minds at his School of Seamanship at a time when the Portuguese got their heads around the *Volta do Mar*: the system of using trade winds to make Atlantic round trips.

Sines; the Cape of Many Battles is Cape St Vincent – but, hey, that's what happens when you're the southwesternmost point of mainland Europe.

Ponte Vasco da Gama: You just went under the huge Golden Gate-like Ponte 25 de Abril suspension bridge, but even that couldn't handle Portugal's traffic, so they decided to build the *second*-longest bridge in Europe alongside it, named after the Portuguese conquistador who rounded the Cape of Good Hope and named Natal (on Christmas Day 1947) as well as being an absolute monster when he reached India.

Lisboa, which in English rhymes with Brisbane.

Ferrel: Will Ferrell is in *Downhill*; the peninsula often mistaken for an island is the fiendish Peniche.

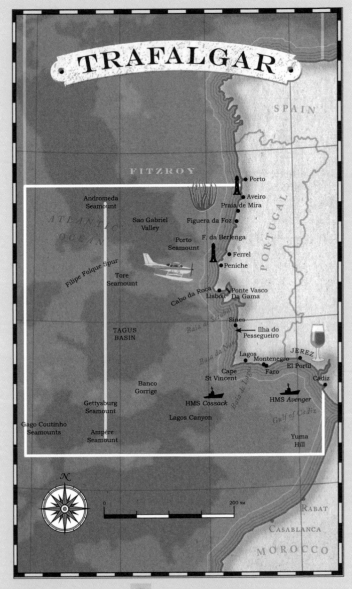

Trafalgar Voyage #2: I ● **316 nautical miles**

A journey requiring enormous valour and stamina, this time with land never in sight: thank your lucky navigational stars that the weather was kind to you.

Andromeda Seamount, which was discovered by Portuguese Hydrographic Survey Ship NRP *Andromeda*; the alpha star of the Andromeda galaxy, Alpheratz, is of course one of the 57 stars of celestial navigation.

Gettysburg Seamount, part of Gorringe Ridge, named after Capt. Henry Honychurch Gorringe of the USS *Gettysburg*, which was once named *Douglas* and ferried passengers between Liverpool and the Isle of Man before being sold to the American Confederacy, then captured by Union forces and renamed just two weeks before Lincoln's Gettysburg Address... which is quoted in the clue.

Ampère Seamount: seamounts are, as the name suggests, mountains which don't quite make it through the surface of the water to become islands or cliff-rocks – in other words, be careful! Seamounts are also of great interest to marine biologists, as they provide 'stepping stones' for the dispersal of species throughout the oceans, and to new-agers, who believe that they contain manmade features, thus proving the existence, once, of... fair Atlantis.

SOLUTION – MAP 19

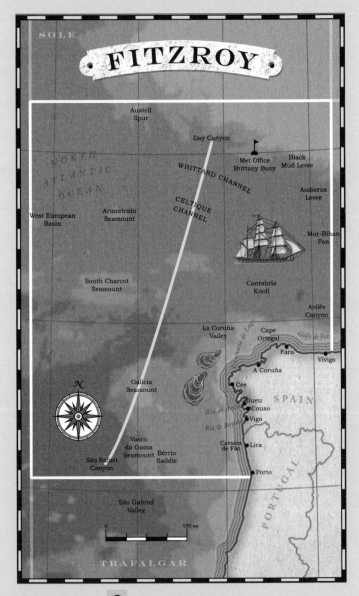

SOLE

FITZROY

Austell
Spur

Day Canyon

Met Office
Brittany Buoy

Black
Mud Levee

NORTH
ATLANTIC
OCEAN

WHITTARD CHANNEL

Audierne
Levee

CELTIQUE
CHANNEL

West European
Basin

Armoricain
Seamount

Mor-Bihan
Fan

South Charcot
Seamount

Cantabria
Knoll

Avilés
Canyon

La Coruña
Valley

Cape
Ortegal

Golfo de Foz

Faro

Vivigo

A Coruña

Galicia
Seamount

Cée

Bueu

SPAIN

Couso

Ria de Aroz

Vigo

Ria de Bayona

Vasco
da Gama
Seamount

Bérrio
Saddle

Cavalos
de Fão

Lira

São Rafael
Canyon

Porto

São Gabriel
Valley

PORTUGAL

0   100 km

TRAFALGAR

Fitzroy Voyage: I ● 424 nautical miles
It was – pretty much – a straight line in the end, pretty much
between the 10th and 11th parallels – and the travel through
the gale was relatively straightforward; Bob FitzRoy would
have approved.

Day Canyon, as represented in the flags of the international code of signals and as named after a geophysicist named Day.

Whittard Channel: from 1886, Walter Whittard of Chelsea began importing tea, though the shops are now a private-equity outfit, and the channel was in fact named after the brilliant Bristol stratigraphist Walter Frederick Whittard.

Celtique seachannel: a French term for 'Celtic'; the auld alliance saw the Scots and the French working together to try to cut down on England's persistent invading.

Galicia Seamount: the ancient Iberian kingdom of Galicia gives its name to this feature.

São Rafael Canyon, and the three top Catholic archangels share a feast day; the *São Rafael* was a three-master which Da Gama ordered to be burned off the coast of Kenya after losing enough crew to scurvy that he could reduce the number of boats.

SOLUTION – MAP 20

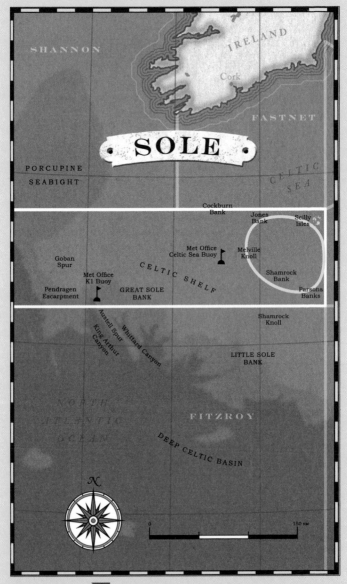

SHANNON

IRELAND

Cork

FASTNET

SOLE

PORCUPINE
SEABIGHT

CELTIC
SEA

Cockburn
Bank

Jones
Bank

Scilly
Isles

Goban
Spur

Met Office
Celtic Sea Buoy

Melville
Knoll

CELTIC SHELF

Met Office
K1 Buoy

Shamrock
Bank

Pendragen
Escarpment

GREAT SOLE
BANK

Parsons
Banks

Shamrock
Knoll

Austell Spur

King Arthur
Canyon

Whittard Canyon

LITTLE SOLE
BANK

NORTH

ATLANTIC

OCEAN

FITZROY

DEEP CELTIC BASIN

N

0   150 NM

Sole Voyage: O ◣ **241 nautical miles**
The *other* voyage that is (almost) quite literally a round trip.

SOLE VOYAGE

Melville Knoll: Herman Melville's *Billy Budd* became Britten's opera aboard HMS *Indomitable*.

Jones Bank: reference to Davy Jones's Locker, euphemism for the seabed; no one is sure why the Sailors' Devil is known as Davy Jones, but my favourite theories include Jonah, and a publican of the same name who kidnapped hapless mariners.

Scilly Isles: the same soundalike means that there's a part of Surrey – whose road system was thought to contain islands that were silly – now depicted on road signs as 'Scilly Isles'.

Parsons Bank: the tellers of tales in fragments of *The Canterbury Tales*.

Shamrock Knoll: Lipton entered the Americas Cup five times with *Shamrock* through *Shamrock V* and received an award as 'The Best of all Losers'.

Melville Knoll again: Peck played Captain Ahab in the 1956 film version of Melville's *Moby-Dick*.

Lundy Voyage: T ▌▌ 242 nautical miles

I hope you enjoyed your views of the Tin Coast. If it's at all reassuring, the land can be just as terrifying. Wilkie Collins was petrified by a walk on the coastal path at Botallack, and *he*'s the man who wrote *The Woman in White*.

St Ives: in the rhyming riddle, we encounter seven wives, 49 sacks (7^2), 343 cats (7^3), and 2,401 'kits' (7^4).

Padstow, reflecting the effect on the village of the various eateries established by fish-devouring chef Rick Stein.

Bude: plucky little GCHQ Bude, from which an undersea cable carried telegrams to and from New Jersey; the shipwreck museum is at the stunning Hartland Quay.

Westward Ho!: the only UK town with an exclamation mark, named after Charles Kingsley's rattling tale of piracy which did wonders for the tourist trade around his nearby home of Clovelly.

The Worm, whose name meant 'dragon' to the Vikings, is a promontory which can get cut off: a young Dylan Thomas fell asleep there and woke up trapped; he described his terror of rats and of 'things I am ashamed to be frightened of '; when little points of reef appeared on the waterline, 'perilously, I climbed along them to the shore'.

Weston-super-Mare: there were so many 'West-Towns' that *this* one decided to assume a fancier name, with hyphens, to stress that it is beside the seaside.

(The) Mumbles: site of a lighthouse that's a classic of the form (because of the thousands of shipwrecks the rocky bay has witnessed); it was on the other side of the water that Coleridge was interrupted while writing up his Kubla Khan dream by that 'Person from Porlock'.

Llanelli: although, of course, in Welsh, 'LL' is a letter in its own right.

Angle, where you can enjoy the sight of plovers, dunlins and Cetti's warblers before visiting the humble and humbling Sailors' Chapel.

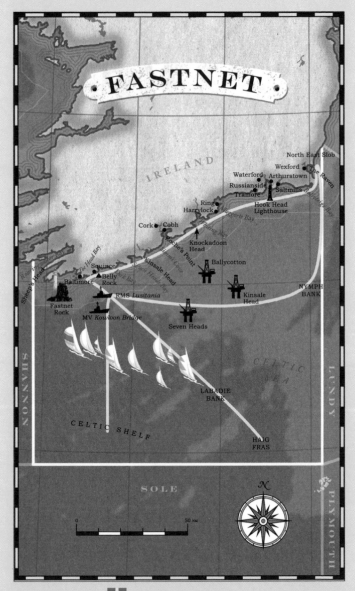

Fastnet Voyage: R ▪ ▪ **482 nautical miles**
You've seen the entire southern coast of the island of Ireland, and
stopped in all three counties, Wexford, Waterford and Cork...
Before you know it, *you'll* be competing in the Fastnet Race.

FASTNET VOYAGE

Celtic Shelf, your bit of the European continental shelf.

MV *Kowloon Bridge* (coordinates for bridge on Kowloon Bay); this carrier was registered in Hong Kong and, weather-damaged in 1986, abandoned then run aground, spilling fuel far and wide.

Nymph Bank: however supernatural, nymphs are well regimented, with Nereids assigned alongside Poseidon, helping sailors like the Argonauts; nowadays, buoys do a similar job.

The Raven, dunes of sea sand blown ashore over the last half-millennium, held in place by plants.

North East Slob: the insulting sense of 'slob' comes from the one it has here: 'muddy land'; this undeniably muddy land is home to 10,000 white-fronted geese.

Saltmills: the mills go back thirteen centuries; more on the hut: 'To the credit of the extreme honesty of the peasantry… nothing of those provisions was ever stolen, though it was notorious that they were there, in an open space, only half a mile distant from the shore.'

Arthurstown (reference to King Arthur's legendary home), where all of the Three Sisters (rivers Barrow, Nore and Suir) gush.

Russianside: that ancient lighthouse – Hook Head – was, like so many others, first built by monks as a fire beacon.

Cork: nearby Cobh offers the 'Titanic Experience' etc.

Squince, where your anchorage is halfway along the haven.

Baltimore, which, like so many other spots, calls its pillar-shaped beacon 'Lot's Wife'.

Haig Fras – anagram ('swimming') of 'a garfish' – granite outcrop teeming with Devonshire cup corals, encrusting sponges and squat lobsters. Enjoy the company!

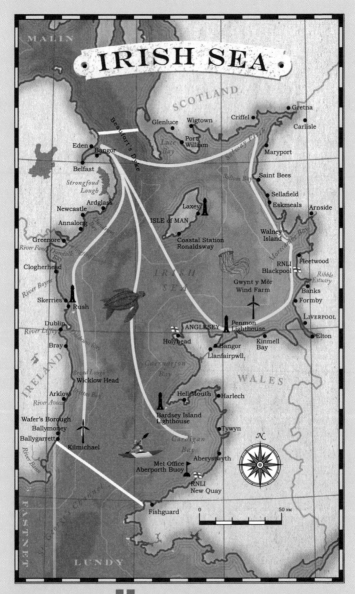

Irish Sea Voyage: R 573 nautical miles

What could have been one of your gentler journeys was
unfortunately blighted by bad luck with the weather, so bravo on
arriving in the sanctuary of Cardigan Bay (unless an orca got in
your way at the end).

Kilmichael ('kill Michael' Corleone, though even the one who actually shoots him doesn't seem to manage this), planned wind-farm site.

Rush; ingots and coins suggest this was a cosmopolitan trading post where mingled Irish, Romans and those of mixed heritage.

Boyne: on 12 July, smartphones across the UK announce Battle of the Boyne day.

Belfast, where the *Titanic* centre recalls the city's Harland & Wolff shipyard.

Criffel ('creel fell'): the Devil let go a lobster pot of rocks, leaving the rabble of hills which look down on the Solway Firth.

Saint Bees: where a local noble offered the shipwrecked nun St Bega as much land as was covered by snow the next morning (in midsummer; this being folklore, snow fell, the nun got a priory and it's now known as Whitehaven); in 1778, this was America's only attempt to invade these islands, it supplied Dublin's tobacco, rum and slaves from the New World and, with its grid, became the inspiration for such cities as New York.

Sellafield, formerly the Windscale two-pile facility; 20 years later, after September 11, every Irish household was issued tablets in case of an attack here.

Morecambe, home town of Eric Morecambe, whose statue is visible from the bay.

Formby: the George Formby statue is in *his* home town of Wigan.

Llanfair PG (or, if you prefer, Llanfairpwllgwyngyllgogerychwyr ndrobwllllantysiliogogogoch), a name which owes more to cunning minds in the tourist office than to geographical features.

Bangor, Gwynedd, immortalised in Fiddler's Dram's 'Day Trip To Bangor (Didn't We Have A Lovely Time)'; the people of Rhyl were outraged by reports that the band were in *fact* inspired by a happy day out in Rhyl but concluded that it lacked a syllable.

Bangor, County Down: they both had a big old wattle fence (*benchoer, beannchar, bennchuir* etc).

Cardigan: where there's a curse on the emerald cave, the Witch's Cauldron.

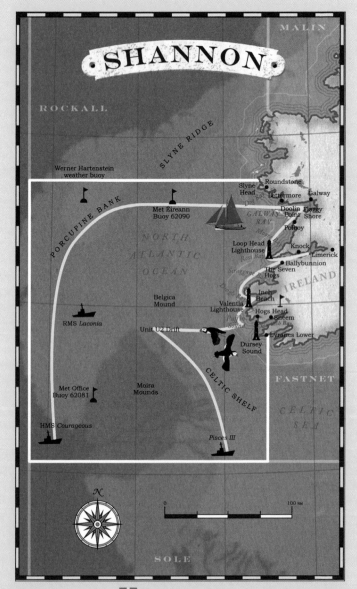

Shannon Voyage: R 🟥🟥 **709 nautical miles**

A sombre starting point, but happily your voyage ends at a point where you can, with *Pisces III* in mind, reflect on those who have coordinated extraordinary things at sea – such as yourself!

SHANNON VOYAGE

HMS *Courageous*, which lies here ignominiously after many years carrying up to 48 aircraft at a time.

Porcupine Bank, home to cold-water coral reefs that may help with medical research and which appear to remain practically unsullied by man (there are no porcupines here; the crew of a paddle-wheel surveying ship called HMS *Porcupine* were the first to announce their discovery of the bank).

Galway Bay (sung by the cops in the chorus of 'Fairytale of New York'... even though there is no NYPD choir) and home to the annual Cruinniú na mBád festival, a race of the handsome transomed local vessels, the Galway hookers.

Flaggy Shore, which Heaney in 'Postscript' urges you to visit 'In September or October, when the wind / And the light are working off each other' – do read the whole poem.

Limerick: in the ninth century, Vikings sailed up the Shannon planning their usual pillaging but the locals sent them back.

Knock, which – being a village of 200-odd inhabitants – is unconnected with Ireland's 'heftier and more famous airport.

The Seven Hogs (imaginary continuation of the *Three Little Pigs* story), known for the clarity of the water.

Inch Beach, to which film-makers needing a spot of 'majestic Erin' return time and again, from *The Playboy of the Western World* (whose art director built a cottage here) to *Ryan's Daughter*.

Puffin Sound; various homes for puffins around the British Isles have been established by solar-powered loudspeakers playing the distinctive growly mating call out to the sea.

Hogs Head Golf Club, which is unlike Hogsmeade's Hog's Head Inn in that the Hog's Head Inn has no staff dedicated to guests who wish to arrive by private jet.

Unit U2 Drift (via reference to U2's guitarist) whose clays contain volcanic glass, obsidian grains and pumice.

Pisces III (astrological symbol, thrice), a submersible used in 1973 for eight-hour shifts of liquefying mud using water jets to lay transatlantic undersea phone cables; *Pisces III* flipped and sank back to the seabed: what became the deepest sub rescue ever undertaken is related in the memoir *No Time on Our Side* (and was successful!).

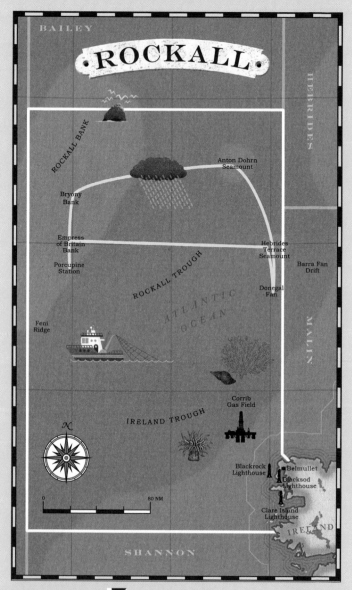

Rockall Voyage: A **379 nautical miles**

However, don't strap on your scuba where you are now, as the *Empress* herself is much closer to shore.

Porcupine Station; laying a transatlantic telegraph cable in the 1860s required a decent survey of the ocean floor; the good people of the paddle-wheeler HMS *Porcupine* passed this way and valiantly tried to climb onto Rockall. Valiantly and vainly, but Commander Hoskyns did manage to scrape off a piece of rock and sent it to an Irish geologist; visit Queen's College, Galway if you want to get a load of the celebrated Hoskyns Specimen.

Bryony Bank, where demersal trawlers have found, appropriately enough, tiny filter feeders known as bryozoan (as well as the odd herring); the garden pest is the ivy-like bryony, which can play havoc with shrubs, beds, hedges, trees and walls.

Anton Dohrn Seamount: Dohrn is famous among naturalists for setting up a 'zoological station': like a railway station, but marine and a place for scientists to stop and carry out experiments. It wasn't out here, obviously, but in balmy Naples; the seamount's name nevertheless reflects the biodiversity under your vessel.

Donegal Fan: fourteen of Friel's plays are set in Donegal's fictional Ballybeg, including the famous ones.

Hebrides Terrace Seamount, once upon a time a volcano. While it's a long way from the Hebrides, Scottish seas have much to thank the Hebrides Terrace for: it diverts the currents in just the right way to give the waters things that fish like to eat, which means fish, which means larger marine mammals, which means a vibrant and diverse underwater world.

***Empress of Britain* Bank**: RMS *Empress of Britain* is of great interest to those who think that when it was torpedoed, it was carrying South African gold to America to pay off war debts; in 1995, explorers found that it did have a bullion room... but instead of gold, there was the skeleton of a salvager. The hunt for the billion-euro booty goes on.

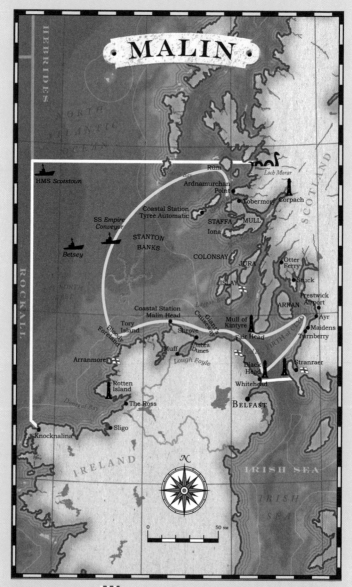

Malin Voyage: G ||| 311 nautical miles

And you never had to negotiate the gargantuan container vessels in the Clyde: this was a generally more 'natural' voyage and one you surely left with fresh ideas; Malin, by the way, is named for Malin Head, which we can translate as, pleasingly, 'Brow Head'

Calgary Bay, though it does have a castle, and gave its name to the Canadian Calgary.

Rùm (which can mean 'strange', and is a brew, and whose spelling was changed to 'Rhum' by its Victorian playboy owner because he didn't want to be known as the boozy 'Lord of Rum'; the 'h' was dropped in 1991), where the white machair of the beaches can make it look as though it's been snowing in August.

Bloody Foreland, which also sounds a *lot* better than the name's literal translation, the ghastly 'Hill of Blood'.

Tory Island (May, Heath and Eden being Tory PMs), which has a lot of tors and which is, um, let's say, an *unconventional* community with a *thriving* arts scene, an 'elected monarch' of sorts, and a sign reading 'PLEASE NOTE THAT TIME HAS NO RELEVANCE ON THE ISLAND'.

Shrove, which pleasingly means 'The Snout'; under the Good Friday Agreement, the 'Loughs Agency' oversees Lough Foyle.

Giant's Causeway, voted the UK's fourth-greatest natural wonder by *Radio Times* readers and established as a set of stepping stones for a punch-up between the enormous Irish giant Finn MacCool and his behemoth Scottish rival Benandonner.

Black Head, which inspired the name of the other headland White Head, which in turn gave *its* name to the town of...

Whitehead, where you can follow the route of Gobbins Path, once a precarious trail above the coast of 'tubular bridges' and the like, concocted by an eccentric Victorian engineer who charged sixpence, and now far, *far* too dangerous to follow on land.

Turnberry, as featured in the *New York Times* investigation 'Where Did Donald Trump Get Two Hundred Million Dollars to Buy His Money-Losing Scottish Golf Club?'

Maidens, Robert the Bruce's entry point after leaving Rathlin Island, before going on to do his not-immeasurable thing.

Ayr, originally known as Inverayr, meaning 'mouth of the Ayr': this coast is the only part of the UK visited by Elvis, when he stopped at Prestwick Airport on his way back from West Germany, having completed his national service.

Mull of Kintyre, a song which Paul McCartney wrote while he was there, pretending that he wasn't.

SOLUTION – MAP 27

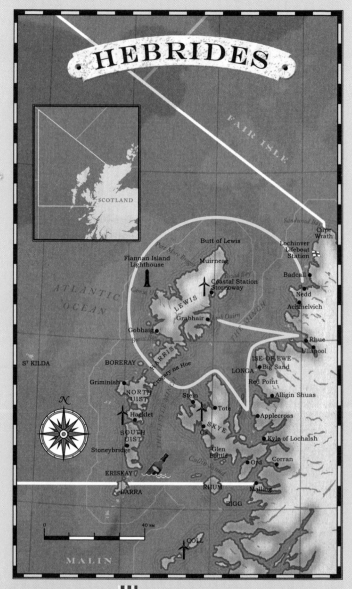

Hebrides Voyage: G ||| 298 nautical miles

You have performed more manoeuvres than you thought possible, and your brain has been repeatedly battered with beauty. I recommend repairing to the *Politician* Lounge Bar on Eriskay.

Nedd, which means 'nest' in the local tongue: when fisherman started using larger vessels at the beginning of the twentieth century, they needed shelter, which the nest of Loch Nedd could offer (reference: *The Simpsons* neighbour Ned Flanders).

Badcall, or rather Upper Badcall and Lower Badcall, where sailors used to be advised to procure a fisherman from one of the cottages northeastward of Leopach Channel and persuade them to act as pilot.

Boreray, part of St Kilda, where there are sadly no bees, and which they call the Island on the Edge of the World; you, however, will be travelling much further out (on *other* pages of this book).

Stein, a crofting village which used to have the splendid name of Lochbay; Skye is the setting for that Virginia Woolf novel mentioned.

Tote, once cleared of people to make room for more sheep.

Applecross (as in, imagined hybrids of Pink Lady with Granny Smith and Golden Delicious with Royal Gala): a village which the locals typically do not call 'Applecross', preferring simply 'The Street'.

Longa Island, an uninhabited former fishing community just half a nautical mile from...

Big Sand, sheltered from the onshore wind by Longa and a very good place to stop and watch the sun set.

Isle of Ewe (say it out loud), whose appropriately named Main House has been inhabited by the same family since the mid-1800s – and they are, in fact, the Isle of Ewe's *only* family.

Rhue ('rue'): the nearby island with the unfortunate sheep is Gruinard, which had 280 tonnes of formaldehyde sprayed on it in the 1980s to try and get rid of all that nasty and fatal anthrax.

Grabhair, which has a handy pier at which you can conclude your Hebridean adventure.

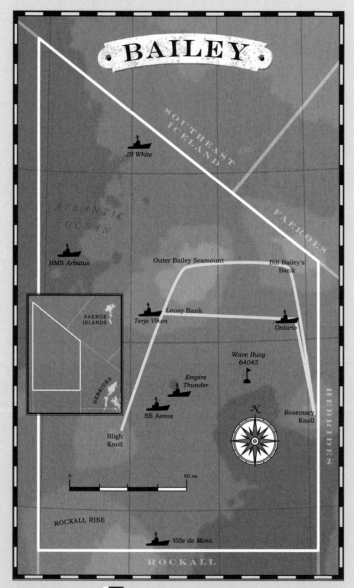

Bailey Voyage: A **380 nautical miles**

You are now the only mariner ever to have undertaken a pleasure trip around Bailey in the fog; dubious distinction is still distinction.

BAILEY VOYAGE

Bligh Knoll: Fletcher Christian seized command of HMS *Bounty* from Captain Bligh in the south Pacific; this bank was discovered by the happier crew of the research vessel RV *George Bligh*, itself named after a commander who was there when Nelson died on HMS *Victory*.

Outer Bailey Seamount: reference to parts of a castle.

Bill Bailey's Bank (music from 'Bill Bailey, Won't You Please Come Home?'); the original Bill Bailey was not a sailor too far from shore, but a barfly, and there is a connection: G.T. Atkinson of the old Ministry of Agriculture and Fisheries describes a Grimsby steam long-liner which discovered the area (and its lucrative halibuts) and how its navigator decided that 'to give it a name nothing seemed better than the popular song of the day'.

Rosemary Knoll: in Act 4 Scene 5 of *Hamlet*, Ophelia says: 'There's rosemary, that's for remembrance; pray, love, remember: and there is pansies, that's for thoughts'; Rosemary Knoll is part of a volcano – happily an extinct one.

Ontario (postal abbreviation ON): this wreck is a trawler attacked by the Luftwaffe; all crew were rescued.

Lousy Bank: reference to successive Plagues of Egypt in Exodus, which some consider part of something they call the Rockall-Faeroe Microcontinent.

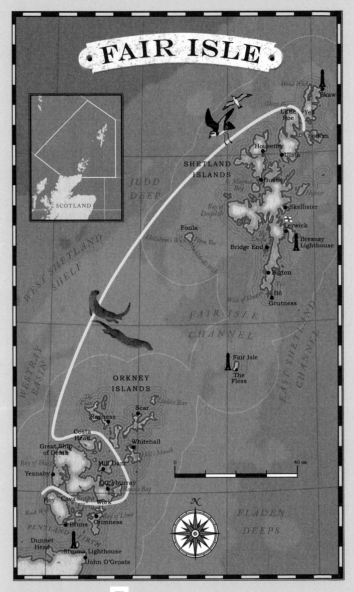

Fair Isle Voyage: S █ 162 nautical miles

170 fair isles, in fact; 171 if you choose to count as an 'isle' the mainland where you have now landed.

FAIR ISLE VOYAGE

Sodom: Hugh MacDiarmid, figure of the Scottish Renaissance, who lived there, was amused at the Ordnance Survey's anglicised version of Suðheim, which itself means nothing more than South Home and pleasingly ignores all that *other* stuff further to the south, like the so-called 'mainland'.

Yell, whose claim to be the Otter Capital of Britain is one you'd be brave to challenge.

Little Roe: so called because it's small and red; that noise you can hear is a 'conversation' among storm petrels.

Great Ship of Death: not actually a 'Ship', more of a cairn, but undeniably 'Great' and, given the remains of 25 crouching people from 5,000-odd years ago, that 'Death' bit of the name is on the money.

Costa Head (as in the irrepressible coffee chain), site in the 1950s of an experimental edifice where propeller blades attached to some steel and a gearbox was connected to the National Grid: look it up if you're interested in the category of Signs of Things to Come.

Work: the causeways mentioned were officially 'improvements to communication', because you mustn't use POWs for a war effort, a subterfuge slightly undermined by naming them the Churchill Barriers ('The Drugs Don't Work'; 'This Woman's Work'; 'Let's Work Together'; 'We Can Work It Out', each an *absolute* banger).

Cava (sparkling wines): the sheltered body is Scapa Flow, longship docking point for the Vikings and chief UK naval base in both the First and the Second World Wars.

Hoy (as in speedy Sir Chris): the name 'Pentland Firth' comes from a Norse word for 'Land of the Picts'; oh, and it's also not *really* a firth...

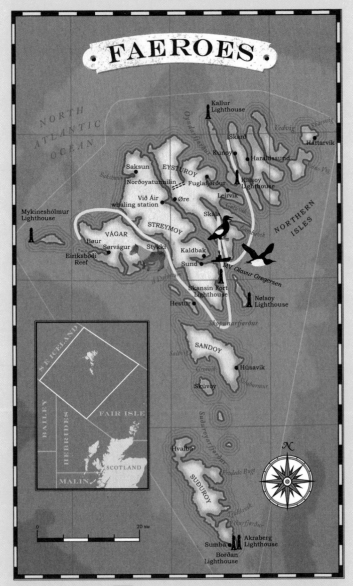

FAEROES

Faeores Voyage: W ▣ **85 nautical miles**

Your opinions welcome on the age-old debate as to whether the name means Sheep Islands or the less intriguing Land Islands; I strongly advise you now to head immediately to Haraldssund or the village of Kunoy itself for some welcoming company.

FAEROES VOYAGE

Bøur (in Faeroese, pronounced very similarly to 'Boer War' and indeed 'boar'), a village which they say was once punished for the 'crime' of taking a piece of burning wood from nearby Sørvágur when Bøur itself had no fire.

Stykki, actually a very dignified spot where you can see some Viking horses (which might make you imagine enormous equines, but which are in fact are really not at all unlike dinky Shetland ponies): its island's name, Streymoy, means 'island of currents', which really should tell you *something* as a navigator.

Sandoy (S and OY) which, it will not surprise you to hear, is the only Faeroe island with, well... dunes (although it can get just as jagged as the rest).

Skála (reference to Milan's La Scala), where you can disembark and marvel at the Fuglafjørður thermal springs or sit and listen to the sky-splitting chatter of the black guillemots.

Skarð ('scarred', not 'bag'), where we end with a dispiriting tale: in 1913, the village had seven able-bodied men in its population, all of whom died at sea at Christmas; the women and children then all moved to Haraldssund; apologies for sharing with you that image, but... life here has *never* been easy.

SOLUTION – MAP 31

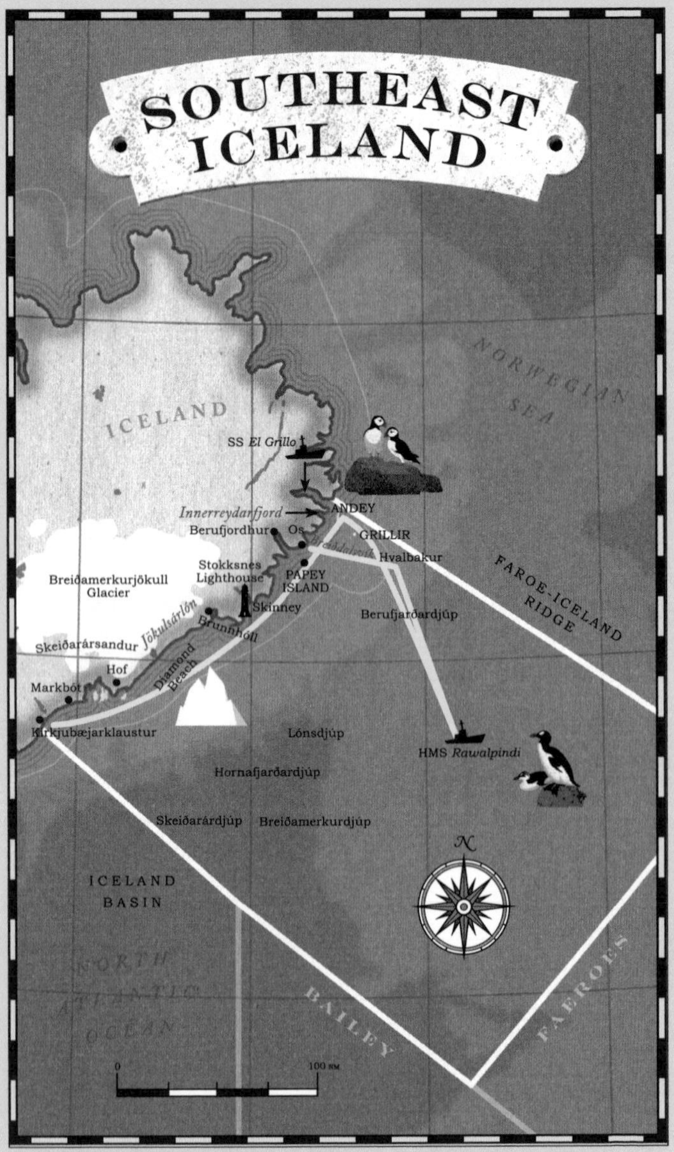

Southeast Iceland Voyage: A  **311 nautical miles**

After all that arctic air descending your lungs and stomach, how about a nice cold glass of *vatnajökull*? Skál!

Kirkjubæjarklaustur (which the locals understandably call Klaustur), where the tops of columns of volcanic rock, all nestled together, form the ground in a way that resembles the paved floor of a church – or at least they do if you're pious; those same Irish monks whose island you pass at the end of this journey set up their pious homes here in the pre-Viking days.

Skinney (as in skinny latte): you're at the edge of a World Heritage site, made of glacial stretches famous for being multi-coloured, for letting lose mini-bergs that give Diamond Beach its name and, importantly, for making up a large part, along with Arctic thyme, of *vatnajökull*, the lovely local beer.

Andey, with reference to mangled Icelandic names of the Bee Gees, an island home to 15,000 pairs of puffins – leave them to breed.

Grillir (reference to the infamous George Foreman Lean Mean Fat-Reducing Grilling Machine), the northernmost point you'll reach in *any of* these voyages and just 15 nautical miles from the very top of all of the Shipping Areas.

HMS *Rawalpindi* of the P&O Fleet, requisitioned by the Admiralty; when her captain – the father of Ludovic Kennedy – spotted two massive German warships here in 1939, his response was intolerably poignant: 'We'll fight them both, they'll sink us – and that will be that. Goodbye.'

Hvalbakur, a skerry which extends Iceland's fishing rights that handy wee bit further (to the chagrin this time of the Faeroese).

Ós; És and Æs are worth the same; an Icelandic Scrabble player feels lucky when he or she pulls the single Ý tile, worth nine points.

YOUR REWARD

You are now a seasoned old salt. You deserve something to acknowledge that.

So, for your final challenge: **use the letters you have gathered to complete the sea shanty below**. Once you've made all the letters into words that fill those gaps, go to penguin.co.uk/shippingforecast to find out the answers – if you're correct, you are worthy of a special Certificate of Maritime Proficiency.

We made our _____ for storms or for gales

_____ this _____ a-speckle with _____

Diverting the weather to work with our _____

_____ on stoutly and heading for home

You've earned it, Cap'n.

The letters you've gathered...

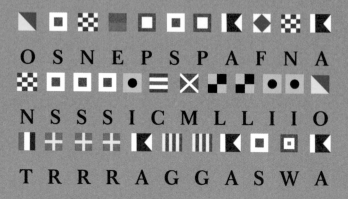

O S N E P S P A F N A

N S S S I C M L L I I O

T R R R A G G A S W A

...can be assembled into the words to
complete the shanty:

CREW

Captain: the indefatigable Albert DePetrillo
of BBC Books

Chief Mates: the steadfast Daniel Sorensen,
Yvonne Jacob and Charlotte Macdonald

Sailing Master: our cartographer Liane Payne

Purser: Andrew Gordon, agent extraordinaire

Surveyors: Steve Tribe, Jonathan Baker, Paul Simpson
and Bobby Birchall

Chief Cooks: Tamara Gilder and Richard Osman

Engine Department: Chief Engineer Andy Bowden
and Engineering Officers Will Chappell, Chris Almond
and Penelope Endersby, all of the Met Office

Electro-Technical Department: Gareth Bellis of the
National Maritime Museum, Mary Mowat of the
British Geological Survey and all the staff at the
Map Room in the National Archives, Richmond
Reference Library, the Archaeology Data Service
and the UK Hydrographic Office

Warrant Officer: Richard Hamilton

Wipers: Mum, Alex, Raphael and Lucy

If you've enjoyed exploring the Shipping Areas,
I recommend *Rain Later, Good* (paintings by
Peter Collyer) and *The Shipping Forecast* (photos
by Mark Power) and the books *Attention All Shipping*,
The Shipping Forecast: A Miscellany and *And Now
the Shipping Forecast*.

These journeys would not have been possible without
the Admiralty Charts, OpenSeaMap, the many
volunteers who have created resources that work within
Google Earth and various editions of the magnificent
Reeds Nautical Manual and the United States
Hydrographic Office *Sailing Directions*.

If you go out there and do it for real, *do* please
disregard all the routes above and *bon voyage*.